What I Need To Know About Living I Learned From My Dogs

Essays on Living

H. D. Johns

ISBN Number 1-57087-438-7

Library of Congress Catalog Card Number 98-67687

Professional Press
Chapel Hill, NC 27515-4371

Manufactured in the United States of America
99 00 01 02 03 10 9 8 7 6 5 4 3 2 1

With love and appreciation to

Bill Ben, Shakti, Tawny, Rags, Kuma, Chiribako, Tina, Tigger, Barney, Poppy, Lacey, Graham, Rusty
and
all the other dogs I have known and loved.

With a special tribute to
Lacey
(12/25/81 - 1/14/97)

Thanks to Donna who encouraged the writing of this book, and to Laura who read, and approved of, the first manuscript.

Contents

1

If I Were A Dog

In writing this book I often thought of what it would be like had I been born a dog. I have come to prefer, as a companion, a quiet and gentle breed such as a Golden Retriever, and I think, if I had the choice, that is what I would decide to be.

Had I been born a Golden Retriever, I would be alert and responsive but quiet, sensible and serene. I would be filled with adoration for those who care for me and I would be friendly to and curious about everyone who comes into my view. I would follow anyone who calls me but my master would not have to call me. I would enjoy being with that person and would follow her from room to room, just because I like to be with her.

I would choose as my favorite toys, lots and lots of tennis balls. In fact, I would consider any tennis ball I saw, whether in a tennis game or just lying on the ground, to be mine and mine alone. If I saw one thrown I would retrieve it but I would have to be trained to give it up without a tug-of-war.

My mouth would be soft and gentle, not given to biting anything but food...

I would show my feelings freely by putting my head between my paws to sulk; by grinning broadly when I am overjoyed; by wagging my tail in anticipation of an event, such as a walk or a ride in the family car; by jumping and turning around rapidly when I am excited by the promise of a romp with a person or with another dog.

I would be patient with children, although I must say that I enjoy the company of playful adults more. My forte would be assisting blind or disabled people.

And, oh yes, I could work as a hunting dog, retrieving waterfowl that have been shot from the sky, but I would prefer chasing tennis balls!

2

About Mortality

One thing that dog owners have to come to terms with is that dogs do not live very long. Small dogs may live to be 17 or 18 years old; large dogs usually die somewhere between 10 and 14. That means that the average dog owner will have to witness the death of a loyal and loving companion about four or five times in 75 years of human life. One who is not familiar with the practice of caring for and loving dogs cannot fathom the heartbreak that comes from the loss of such a friend. As you see your faithful dog grow older and become gray and/or arthritic, anxiety begins to grow in anticipation of the pending loss.

My own experience with the death of a dog began when I was twelve years old. My father bought an

Airedale when I was born. His name was Bill Ben. In the small town where I grew up, Bill was my constant companion, going with me to the post office and to the candy store. He even accompanied me to school. There was a band of gypsies who summered in our village and I could walk by their encampment bravely with Bill Ben at my side.

One morning Bill Ben was not at his usual spot before the door on the front porch. I went to look for him and found him lying at the side of the garage, dead. For weeks afterward I dreamed of the dog. I missed him terribly and could not understand the loss.

The anxiety about death transferred to the knowledge that human beings, too, are mortal. I became particularly anxious about my father. My mother was killed in an automobile accident when I was three years old. My father was both mother and father to me and I became obsessed with the idea that he, too, would someday die. As a teenager I used to pray that I would die before my father.

When I was 23 years old my father died. I noticed with surprise that I experienced not only the sadness of loss, I also experienced a kind of relief. Relief from the anxiety of impending death.

For some time I had noticed my anxiety about Lacey, my Golden Retriever, as she approached the ripe old age of thirteen years, on Christmas Day 1994. I began giving her special attention, to ward off any guilt I might have following her passing. In fact, my anxiety got in the way of my enjoying brushing and stroking her.

Thinking about my earlier experiences with death I began to associate two things: anxiety and relief. And I realized that along with my grief there would come a sense of relief. I would no longer have to worry about her getting old, perhaps becoming crippled or blind or deaf or any of the myriad of maladies that afflict the aging dog.

That awareness helped. I no longer dread with such pain her passing from this world and I can stroke her now and enjoy her being alive and with me. I no longer feel the injustice that such a devoted animal should have such a short life. In a sense all of us have short lives, measured by the span of centuries that the earth has been in existence. So Lacey is teaching me something about mortality: that all lives must come to an end sometime. And that it is something to be faced not only with anxiety, but also with a sense of relief; that the struggle will be over and peace will reign where turmoil and apprehension once held sway.

3

About The Indifference Of Nature

I have a new puppy. I got her at the pound. She is a Briard Shepherd mixed with Chow-Chow and her name is Graham. She is about six months old.

A few days ago I was sitting in my back garden and Graham came running to me playfully tossing something in the air and shaking it. She laid at my feet a dead baby bird and stood there wagging her tail and expecting a reward for fetching. She was happy to be bringing me something she had found...and killed.

The first thought that occurred to me was that "nature is cruel." But then it occurred to me that it is not so much that nature is cruel but rather that nature is indifferent: indifferent to the suffering of her constituent parts. Nature survives on nature.

> *Great fleas have little fleas upon their backs to bite 'em,*
>
> *And little fleas have lesser fleas, and so ad infinitum.*
>
> *And the great fleas themselves, in turn, have greater fleas to go on;*
>
> *While these again have greater still, and greater still, and so on.*
>
> *Augustus De Morgan*
> *(1806-1871)*

Such thinking led me to consider "man's inhumanity to man." When we go to war as a nation are we being cruel or are we being indifferent to the suffering of the men, women, children and animals that are maimed and killed?

And what about the senator who is quoted as saying, "Chickens are raised to be eaten, that is their sole purpose in life." And the millions of cattle and sheep and hogs that go to slaughter to satisfy our human craving for meat.

Take it further: Does a beet mind being eaten? Or a cauliflower being consumed? We live on nature and nature lives off of us. I once visited Hart Island, in Long Island Sound, and saw the lush vegetables being grown on the burial ground of the indigent dead from New York City.

And at last we come to consider the nature of that which created all of our universe. Is God indifferent to suffering?

Well, if you believe in one creative force, not two, then you are forced to an awareness that the same force that created the beauty of nature, the dependability of the universe, love and warmth and caring, is also the source of the ugliness of nature, the whimsicality of the universe and the capacity for hatred and coldness and indifference. It is not that the so-called acts of God are cruel, it is that they are indifferent to suffering. It is as though God has bigger fish to fry than worry about one person or thirty thousand people killed in floods or earthquakes. It is like he set up the rules of the universe, the movement of the planets, the evolution of the species, the usual balances of heat and cold, day and night, winter and summer, and now turns his back on the consequences.

And this leads to the recent interest in the efficacy of prayer. When Eddie Rickenbacker's plane went down in the Pacific Ocean in World War II, he said that he prayed and God sent a bird that landed on his shoulder to provide him with food and liquid. Two questions occur to me: one, if God sent a bird why didn't he send a fat goose instead of an albatross, which is almost inedible and two, what about the thousands of fighting men who prayed and were killed?

Recently an American Pilot was shot down over hostile country. After six days he was rescued and his comment was, "I know that it was the prayers of the American People that saved my life." It makes me sad that he gives God and prayer the thanks instead of claiming his own quick-wittedness and giving the heroic bravery of his rescuers the credit for his salvation. It makes me even sadder to think of the mothers and fathers who have prayed earnestly for the safety of their service sons only to be told, "The Defense Department regrets to inform you...." The plausible explanation is that God is indifferent as to how things work out. God takes no hand in rescues. We wonder if God is pleased that the airman got out safely.

This does not mean that we should not pray, if we believe in it, for the recovery and the safety of our loved ones. In prayer we lift up our hearts and thoughts to the highest compassion and the highest values that we hold. That, it seems to me, is a worthwhile practice. The church has followed the leading of the New Testament in making provision for unanswered prayer: "Nevertheless Lord not my will but thine be done," provides a loophole to keep our faith intact in case of failure.

And if it turns out that it is God's will that one should suffer disease or suffering or death, what does it say about God? That he is cruel? No, I think it says that God is indifferent to human problems.

Why nature is constructed to be indifferent to suffering is an unsolvable dilemma. We have to learn to struggle with it and we have to learn to live with it. It may have some presently undefinable purpose.

Without any conclusive proof you can choose one of two ways to think about life: either it arose by accident and continues to evolve by accident or it is purposive. For me, the weight of evidence points away from accidental selection and toward purposeful selection. I choose to believe that nothing is accidental, that on the contrary, all things have purpose. Often I do not see the immediate purpose. Almost never do I comprehend the long-range purpose.

So, I choose to believe that there may be purpose, even in the indifference to suffering that I see all through nature. And while I am choosing to believe that, my young, happy puppy drops another dead bird at my feet!

4

About Being Childlike

Dogs are very much like children. Both start out in life strictly governed by the Pleasure Principle. They want what they want when they want it. And through a series of frustrating experiences they move gradually toward the Reality Principle. Children learn this by being allowed to take some responsibility for their own behavior. Dogs learn it through consistent reinforcement: disapproval of unacceptable behavior and praise when they conform to the master's standards. In a way dogs, too, thus take responsibility for their behavior.

There are other similarities between dogs and children among them, imagination, spontaneity and awareness.

Imagination means having a mental image of a situation that is not yet in existence or never before perceived. A child sees that a truck, stuck in a low-hanging underpass, could move if some air is let out of its tires. My puppy carries a tennis ball to the top of a stairway, looks down, and imagines what will happen if she drops the ball over the top riser. It will roll to the bottom where she can retrieve it and do it over again.

Spontaneity is an expressed feeling or behavior that occurs without external restraint. A child acting impulsively in accord with internal feelings breaks into a smile when his mother hides her face behind her hand and then peeks out around it, or gurgles when he is pleased. A puppy picks up anything and everything he finds lying around and checks it out in his mouth. He barks immediately when someone rattles the front door of his home.

As for awareness, try to conceal a package behind your back at Christmas time as you move across a room where a child is watching his favorite television show. Try to pick up and dispose of a soiled tennis ball that your snoozing dog has laid aside. In both cases you will be rewarded with at least a questioning glance.

All three of these child-like characteristics are of value in enjoying life. They lend variation and spice to otherwise sometimes tedious lives. Parent figures tend to discourage them in the growing child so that by the time teenage years roll around the child has lost much of his imagination, a lot of his spontaneity and most of his awareness. The average teenager exercises very little imagination in solving problems, is governed by internal and external pressures rather than spontaneity and is barely aware of the people around him or the surrounding environment.

The dog continues to exercise all three of them, or at least the latter two, spontaneity and awareness. In order to be more like dogs in this respect, much of modern group psychotherapy is designed to restore these three magical elements to the adult psyche.

5

About The Enjoyment Of Small Things

One day I gave my five-month-old puppy a large red grape. She mouthed it, spit it out and it rolled across the floor. She immediately jumped after it, pushed it with her foot and jumped high in the air as it rolled away. From then on, it was a picnic, with Graham picking the grape up in her mouth, tossing it in the air, chasing it, rolling it with her foot and scampering about happily and finally, eating it. After that I occasionally give her another grape and each time it is a repeat performance, the puppy dancing about gaily, enjoying the grape. She gets excited when I hold the grape out to her.

Those who keep and care for dogs know with what anticipation a dog looks forward to a walk. Sometimes I take them to a lake where they can roam about in and out of the water. At other times I take them to a park where they can meet other dogs and chase squirrels and birds and tennis balls. And sometimes I just take them around the block. They anticipate the going for a walk by my words, "Let's take a walk," or perhaps by my changing into my walking shoes. Their tails go up, wagging fiercely, they get excited and watch me closely, their eyes shining.

Watching my puppy play with the grape, a friend remarked, "It takes so little to make her happy!"

Now I, too, am beginning to appreciate the small good fortunes that come my way. The cooing of doves in the mornings, the touch of warm water in the shower, the voices of friends on the telephone, a patch of sunlight on a cloudy day, a twenty-minute nap after lunch, a blue sky, the amazing assortment of green colors in nature.

Part of the enjoyment is the element of surprise. To be awakened by the singing of birds each morning still holds surprise for me, seeing a Pileated Woodpecker flashing by, or noticing a bee on a petunia, or feeling a splash of rain on my face when I didn't expect it. It's like the puppy with her first experience with a grape. And part of the enjoyment is in anticipation: looking for a rainbow during a summer shower, looking forward to the first taste of coffee in the morning, waiting for the conductor to mount the podium at a concert, so many of these little things are enjoyed in anticipation of the main event.

And, of course, part of the secret of a happy life is learning to appreciate the part that anticipation plays. I'm sure the dogs are happy when they are walking with me, but they are even more delighted when they are anticipating the walk.

One way to keep life enjoyable is always to have something to anticipate. Is your job boring? Learn to anticipate something pleasant about your arrival at work, perhaps being greeted by a colleague, perhaps sharing a donut or a cup of coffee before you begin work, and perhaps finishing a tedious piece of work. If nothing else, you can anticipate the coming coffee break or the fact that lunch hour is only four hours away. Do you dread the commute home in the evening? Think of the comfort of the big chair, or the relationship you can have with your spouse or your children or your dog!

I have learned to anticipate changing into more casual clothing at the end of the day; to anticipate the good feeling of my mouth after brushing my teeth; and when I am surprised by some small thing unexpectedly entering my horizon, to savor the thrill of the marvelous and changing world.

Like the dog, I wag my tail in anticipation, and I find joy in the surprise of the unexpected.

6

About Intelligence

Years ago, as an undergraduate student, I wrote a paper in which I argued that within one standard deviation of the mean of intelligent quotient, the intelligence factor was not as important as the temperament of the individual involved.

Recently, my experience with dogs has tended forcefully, to bring this idea back to my attention. My older dog, a Golden Retriever, is reasonably intelligent, I think. She has never required any form of punishment, learning the basic obedience commands quickly and submitting unfailingly to them. She learned to sit, lie down, heel, be quiet and fetch on command at an early age. Lacey has also been, by temperament, submissive rather than aggressive or assertive.

My younger dog is also intelligent, highly intelligent I think. I judge this by the rapidity with which she learned basic commands. In less than five minutes she learned to sit and to lie down on command. She caught on quickly to returning a thrown object, a ball or a stick. Sometimes, as I am teaching her to heel, she walks quietly by my left side. But there is a difference. By temperament Graham is assertive and often aggressive.

So there are times when, bombarded by other stimuli such as a squirrel, or a bird, a falling leaf or even an insect flying or crawling along the ground, that Graham refuses to obey any command. At first, this led me to believe that she was not intelligent. Then, I wondered if she were hyperactive with an attention deficit, and this finally led me to an awareness that she was of a different temperament than Lacey. If I accept the premise that both dogs are about equal in their intelligence quotients, it may be that the difference in temperament makes all the difference in the way they react to stimuli.

Now comes a book, *Emotional Intelligence*, (Bantam Press,) by Daniel Coleman, expressing the idea that when it comes to predicting an individual's success, results of I.Q. and Achievement testing may be less productive than the qualities of emotion that are developed by one's experiences from childhood AND the way the biological neural pathways within one's psyche are constructed, i.e., one's temperament.

The difference in intellect and temperament might be illustrated by my sleep being interrupted in the middle of the night by a loud noise. I awaken with some anxiety, perhaps even terror, because of the action of my neural pathways. Then my intellect takes over as I realize that it is the telephone ringing.

My task in training Graham is to allow her intellect to emerge, however, slowly, after something has stimulated her nerve-reaction. I can do this by gently speaking to her and stroking her. Hopefully, the time sequence between the nervous reaction and the intellectual response will gradually become shorter. I doubt that it will disappear completely.

All of this helps me understand human beings. Aggressive behavior is usually a biological response to nerve impulses rooted in a sensation of threat: fear/anxiety. The old saying, "Count ten before you act!" makes sense. It allows time for the intellect to take over the motor responses to what is feared. When I am feeling aggressive or compulsive, or when I am faced with an aggressive action by another person (or a dog), let time-delay be a part of my response.

Temperament serves a worthwhile purpose in all of life. It keeps animals alert to pleasure and to danger. Without it self-preservation as well as enjoyment would not be possible. It is natural and usually self-protective to jump when one hears a threatening noise. It is life-enriching to salivate when one thinks of a chocolate drop or a juicy steak. It is self-fulfilling to respond to a sexual stimulant. Intellect helps us jump in the right direction, teaches us that gratification delayed enhances the result and makes us aware of the consequences of our self-gratifying behavior.

There are two reactions to any stimulus. One is to adapt, the other is to defy. Both of these reactions are born in our temperament. Both are involuntary. Most of us have enough intelligence to make decisions rather than act on impulse. Both intelligence and temperament are important. What happens most of the time is that the intelligence of a given person is not so important as his application of it to his temperament.

7

About Sleeping

My father studied until one o'clock each morning and arose at five o'clock each day. I can hear his voice at six o'clock saying, "Boys, boys," meaning "It's time to get up." For years I had felt guilty about sleeping past my father's morning timing. I usually go to bed about eleven and get up about six-thirty. So I sleep about one-third of the time.

Then, someone called my attention to the fact that dogs sleep a lot of the time and I began to notice just how much time my dogs sleep. I estimate that it is between 18 and 20 hours a day. Think of the wasted time they spend in sleep. Seventy-five to eighty percent of the day!

But what would they be doing if they were not sleeping? In an average day they spend about two minutes eating, they play for a couple of hours in thirty-minute segments, they roam around the fenced-in back yard for an hour and they take a walk of thirty-minutes or so. They neither read nor watch very much television. They listen to music, I suppose, when the hi-fi is turned on, but if they are listening, they are listening with their eyes closed.

I, on the other hand, have many duties to perform. First, I must take care of them. Then I must take care of myself. Then I must take care of the business of the day, ranging from my professional hours to cleaning house, raking leaves, grocery shopping and going to the bank. In the evening, I sometimes take care of other people's needs and desires. Since I am semi-retired, I listen to music and read a lot and, oh yes, I work crossword puzzles. Altogether I spend about ten hours each day, bathing, eating, working and playing and walking the dogs, which, together with sleeping, leaves me with six and one-half hours of time unaccounted in a usual day. So what might I do with some of that time? I might just sit and think and do nothing, or I might contemplate nature or I might take a nap for twenty-minutes or an hour.

For years I had difficulty in dealing with time-out from doing something. Now my reasoning tells me that, if dogs can do it, I can too. I can utilize my spare time to do nothing but sit and think or watch the birds and squirrels in my back yard, or take a nap. Of course it won't be for twenty-hours a day. Dogs do not have the same kinds of responsibilities as humans. But it may be for twenty-minutes, or a half-hour or an hour that I can rest.

Thinking along these lines, my thoughts went back to my father and his punctual use of time. My memory had failed to cope with my guilt about over-sleeping. For, in fact, I now recall that every afternoon my father took a nap. I had recalled that he slept only four hours each night. I had forgotten that every afternoon he took a nap, a long nap, as much as two hours! Not every afternoon, of course. Sometimes he had appointments or duties to observe. But usually, between two and four o'clock in the afternoon he could be found peacefully napping.

And from there my thoughts went to the farmers I knew long ago before electric lighting had invaded the rural areas. Farmers went to bed soon after dark and they got up with the dawn. That sounds like not much sleep at first until one considers that, especially in the wintertime, nights are long! And I made up this little rhyme:

The farmer gets up with the dawn,
Sometimes at half-past three.
But he goes to bed when his work is done,
And he gets more sleep than me!

So now I take a nap now and then, whenever I feel like it and there is time available, and sometimes I just sit and do nothing but think and watch what is going on around me.

I may not be asleep. My dog is lying by my bed or my chair. She may not be asleep either, but she is snoring!

8

About Love As Affection

"I love" is most certainly an ambiguous phrase. It has so many different shades of meaning. It can mean anything from "I like" to "I am enraptured;" from "I have goodwill" to "I am deeply involved in the happiness and contentment of...." from "I am sexually stimulated" to "I cherish our moments together."

In fact the Greeks had four words for "love:" *agape, phileo, eros* and *storge.* Most people are pretty well versed in the meaning of Agape, "goodwill," Phileo, "brotherly (or familial) love" and Eros, "sexual excitement," and not at all aware of Storge, which translates as "affection."

As I write this in my study, my beautiful Golden Retriever, "Lacey" is lying close to me. If I move to my office, very soon I will hear her coming down the stairs to be with me. When I go outside, she follows me through the door. She has affection. She wants to be with me. Affection is the major component of the term "love," that is manifested in a dog's relationship to people.

Usually we are attracted into a permanent commitment to another by Eros. Something about the other person triggers our hormonal flow and we become sexually excited by our thoughts about the "loved" object. It may lead to marriage or a long-term commitment. The advertising media exploits eros by posing beautiful people in commercials and promising successful romantic interludes if we use the advertised product. The other three kinds of love are not calculated to make us want to buy anything and so advertising largely neglects them.

When religion speaks of love it usually is in terms of Agape: "goodwill." The Golden Rule may be interpreted as "Have the same goodwill toward others as you would like others to have toward you." At its most perfect manifestation it means a kind of thoughtful consideration for others that is not diluted by ill will shown to me. In a lesser form it may appear with any of the other three Greek concepts of love.

Phileo is the kind of caring experienced among blood relatives, mothers and fathers and children and cousins and other family members. "Blood is thicker than water," means that family members have a kind of regard for each other that is not found among strangers. "Philadelphia" is the "City of Brotherly Love."

And so we come to Storge. Affection is normally felt in the beginnings of sexual excitement, sometimes in familial relationships and even occasionally in feelings of goodwill. Affection is the kind of love that grows. If a relationship is to endure, it is imperative that as sexual excitement ebbs, affection develops. Affection means, essentially, "I like to be with..."

Agape gets to be routine and is often felt as an obligation. Phileo grows thin at times under the stresses of family disagreements. Eros grows into boredom. (Consider how much less interesting it is the 75th time you see your lover unclothed.) Storge holds people and people, and people and dogs, together in a firm and lasting bond.

I am glad that Lacey likes to be with me because I like to be with her.

9

About Love As A Feeling

Watching the dog move from patient to patient in a hospice, I became aware of the importance of touching and being touched. The dog seemed to sense what was needed, for as she came close to each person, she nuzzled against a leg or an outstretched hand and in return was stroked by each patient, most of whom were smiling as they touched. It was obvious that feeling was being transmitted between the parties involved.

No one has ever defined love adequately (the Greeks came closest to it with their four-way definition) but almost everyone relates to it as a feeling. When someone says to me, "I love you," even when it is accompanied by an embrace, I am not always certain which of the four constituent Greek elements or combination of them is being conveyed. "I like you! " has a clearer meaning. It says "there is something about you that sits well with me!" For that reason, I like "I like..." better than "I love..." in most relationship situations. It is easier to translate. It sounds more down to earth and realistic. I often suggest the substitution of "I like you" for "I love you" to couples who purport to be "in love."

Most of us know what it feels like "to be in love" because we have experienced it. We are overwhelmed by the attraction to another person, so that we want and need that person to satisfy our yearning. We see things we hadn't seen before. The beauty of trees and flowers and skies and clouds. We hear things we had missed before. The ripple of a stream and the song of birds. We go into rich fantasies of close embraces. We smell the perfume of budding trees and grasses. We feel transported to a richer, fuller existence, buoyed up by the warmth of a glance or an endearing word.

The primary attracting force of being in love is usually sexual and here, above all, the emphasis is on our need. We feel we must have a close relationship to him or to her in order to feel that we are complete in ourselves. That feeling is often experienced as "jealousy" which is a mixture of fear-threat and need. The fear of losing a loved person seems always to heighten the sense of need. It is obvious that people feel more intensely and obsessively in love when it is not reciprocated than when it is taken for granted.

Many of us know, again from experience, what loving *feels* like. Sometimes it communicates solace or reassurance when we are feeling discomfort or anxiety. Sometimes it comes as an ache in our upper torso when we feel it for someone who is suffering acutely or chronically and we say we would be willing to substitute ourselves for our suffering friend or loved one. It sometimes comes in the form of anxiety, particularly late at night while waiting for a son or daughter to return from an evening out with friends. It sometimes comes in the form of a rush of tenderness when a baby or a child or a handicapped person comes into the focus of our attention. It sometimes comes in the form of pity when we see or hear of disenfranchised people in our locality or elsewhere in the world.

The feeling of loving is associated with need. The dog seemed to sense that she was needed by the dying patients, and she in a way not dissimilar needed to know that what she was doing was worth the effort. Needing and being needed are worthy components of almost all of our love feelings. When needing and being needed are met with positive responses there is a boost to our self-image.

Defining the word may be a stimulating mental activity but describing the feeling of loving and of being in love is more accurate and far more satisfying. For, after all, love is not a thing to be defined. It is a feeling to be experienced in both fear and joy. Dogs don't understand the word, "love," but it is clear that they know something about the feeling.

10

About Suffering

It is sometimes difficult to know when a dog is hurting. You can tell more from the way they look at you than from their vocal behavior. When a dog is in pain it shows in their eyes. Sometimes they protect an injured paw or rub a front foot across a painful ear, but unless the hurt is traumatic or sudden they don't make a noise about it. And when it is frightful they don't make a lot of noise, just a bit of a whinny, panting or a slight groan. The exception to that is when a noise hurts their ears such as a bell ringing or a siren sounding. Then they howl. But howling is not so much an announcement of suffering as it is an assertion that 'this thing must stop!' or perhaps they are trying to sing along!

In contrast some people like to complain about their ailments. I, for one, seldom suffer long in silence. Not that I read a laundry list of my ailments. I am not like the old gentleman who is said to enjoy his illness. But I know that if I let people know that I hurt they may add in some way to my comfort.

I want to know when my dog hurts. Part of that is the knowledge that she can't describe in words what is bothering her. Part of it is my compassion for all mute animals. Mostly, however, it seems to me that I want to know just because she doesn't complain out loud.

I also want to know when a member of my family or a friend hurts. But I don't want constantly to be reminded of the details: just where and how much they are suffering. If someone has a headache it is important that I know it. It is equally important that I not be reminded of it every hour.

I seldom have a headache. My hurts revolve around my hands: a screwdriver slips or a hammer hits the wrong "nail;" or my legs: I'm always barking my shins. Right now, my dog having tripped me so that I fell on my right hand injuring my little finger, I have a very sore third-knuckle. It hurts when I pick up a book or a pan. I am even reminded of it as I type this essay. How often should I complain about it? I am tempted to say, "Gee, my hand hurts," every time I feel a bit of pain. And what I am seeking, in return, is an acknowledging word of comfort. "Honey, I'm sorry about your finger!" That response gets old and worn out and ineffective after a short while.

I think I've learned from my dogs. Now, instead of voicing my complaint, I just look up at the person closest to me and let my eyes tell them how much it hurts. I have found that I can look very sad and doleful. Of course, that wears thin too, after awhile, but in the meantime it is a welcome relief to the other person's ears and if, done with enough dramatic effect, may warrant the same kind of hug that I give to my dogs when they look at me that way!

11

About "Tough Love"

Lacey, my Golden Retriever was afraid of thunder. I say, "was afraid" She is still afraid, but her behavior, during thunderstorms has changed. She has always shown anxiety when the barometric pressure drops and thunderclouds gather. She used to tremble violently and pant heavily when lightning flashed and loud claps of thunder rolled. Three times she had climbed the five-foot fence surrounding our backyard and ran away in terror. That was before our trip to Pennsylvania.

Three years ago we stayed at Springwoods, a Bed & Breakfast Inn, just outside of Reinholds, Pennsylvania, run by Sandra Gill and her mother, Helen Rader. Since the place welcomed dogs as well as people, Lacey was with us. We arrived about six o'clock in the evening. As we drove into the entrance we noticed that the sky was darkening with the threat of a severe storm. We were considering canceling our dinner reservation in a nearby club because we were afraid that Lacey might run away in fear.

Helen reassured us that she could handle Lacey with no difficulty. She had a small, friendly Shitzu. The little Yuki and our big Lacey were getting along splendidly so we left the two women and the two dogs and went to dinner.

While we were eating the storm erupted violently: winds blowing, thunder crashing, rain coming down in a torrential cloudburst. We ate our dinner in fear and trepidation at what was going on back at Springwoods.

When finally, we returned, the house was lighted by lamps and candles, the electricity being cut off by the storm. By then, the weather had returned to normal and we were met at the entrance by Helen and Sandra and the little Shitzu and Lacey, the latter two with tails wagging.

Helen explained that Lacey had lain like a serene queen at her feet while she wrote some letters by lamplight. I asked her how she had managed.

She said that her little dog had once been afraid of storms, too. That she had attended a lecture by a dog-psychologist three years before, and in a question and answer period had told the expert about her little dog's fear.

"When she is afraid, what do you do?" asked the psychologist.

"I pick her up and try to comfort her by talking softly and stroking her, and giving her a treat," she replied.

"So, you are rewarding her fear by coddling her! What you need to do is demand of her that she be quiet and stop trembling, not even touching her until she obeys you."

"So," said Helen, "The next time it thundered and my little dog went into her hysterical state, I drew myself up and with all of the sternness I could muster, shouted at her, 'That's enough! Stop that right now!' And it worked! After two or three storms, the little dog no longer reacted with such frenzied fear.

"And that's what I said to Lacey tonight. I shouted, 'That's enough! Stop it!' and she settled down and became comfortable enough to lie by my chair as I wrote."

We tried it and while Lacey still gets anxious when it thunders, she no longer becomes unmanageable.

Using the same technique of "tough love" with a puppy who has been abused and is afraid of people, I have learned that forcing her to obey a simple command, that she knows, such as "sit" or "lie down" or "quiet" tends to calm her and stop her shying away, or her aggressive behavior.

As with dogs, so with people. Discipline is best when it comes from within. Failing that kind of internal development, "tough love" must be applied from without until its value has been learned.

When we left Springwoods, Lacey had a toy turkey leg, a gift from Yuki which she still treasures, but more than that she had a gift from Helen: a new method of coping with an old established fear!

12

About Saying, "Thank You!"

Almost every morning I get down on the floor with my ancient Golden Retriever and pet her. Sometimes I massage her hindquarters where she has a touch of arthritis. Then I move to her ears and her chin and finally, when she rolls over on her back, I gently stroke her abdomen. At other times I am in a hurry and I just bend down and touch her ears or her muzzle. No matter how much or how little I pat her she always says, "thanks" by kissing my hand with her tongue.

Like most people I learned as a child to say, "thank you," when I receive a sizable gift. A friend brings me a jar of jelly or a package of shelled pecans and I thank the one who gives it. But frequently I missed the less tangible things that people contributed to my life. I entertain at dinner and my guest picks up her own plate and takes it to the kitchen. I used to protest such behavior, saying, "leave it alone, I'll get it."

Or someone gives me a compliment on the tie I am wearing. It used to be that I would pass off the compliment by telling them where I got it or by denying that it is so beautiful.

Several years ago, after an excellent dinner at the home of a friend, I was served a piece of German Chocolate Cake. Now German Chocolate Cake is my favorite of all cakes and this was the best German Chocolate Cake I had ever tasted. I said as much to the hostess.

She replied, "Oh I just got it out of a box. It's a mix!"

After that rebuff of my compliment I had to work harder to get my point across. "Allow me to say what an extraordinary person your are," I said, "to find such a delicious chocolate cake in a box!"

To which she replied, "Well, thank you!"

I learned from Lacey not to allow the slightest opportunity to pass me by without expressing some form of appreciation. Now when someone takes her own plate to the kitchen after eating, I say, "thank you." And when someone pays me a compliment, I respond with "thank you."

Further I have learned to accept personal favors that used to go unnoticed. When a person I love touches me, or does me some small favor, I smile at them and let them know that I accept their touch and value their behavior. In a manner of speaking, I am licking the hand that feeds me!

13

About Positive Stroking

The abuse of animals ranges from cruelty to benign neglect. We hear a lot about abuse these days: child abuse, spousal abuse, the maltreatment of older people and minorities. We are troubled by man's inhumanity to man and inhumanity to animals. My thoughts plunged deeply into this matter a few months ago when I observed the behavior of my adopted eight-week-old stray puppy who obviously had been ill-treated, either by physical means or by neglect. The young dog was particularly fearful of certain men and of some children because she was afraid. She growled aggressively when confronted with people who somehow threatened her. How to go about changing her unwelcome behavior?

Thinking about it I decided that it was important to put first things first. It was important, of course for her to follow the rules of good behavior. To do that it was necessary for her to learn that most people are her friends and can be trusted. It seems to me that these go hand-in-hand. Since I believe that all emotional problems of human beings or animals stem from a sense of low self-worth, I thought it necessary to begin with that. And how do you build self-esteem? By reinforcing positive behavior with stroking.

So often with fractious dogs, we want to enforce the rules and we grow short-tempered and confrontational when a principle is at stake. Sometimes the self-image of the dog is more important than the principle involved. At such times it is best to reinforce that self-image.

Abuse does not have to be extreme to have a dire effect. I once had two Dachshunds, Tina, the mother and, Tigger, the son. When I would return from a trip I would be met at the door by two delightful dogs prancing up to me, their tails high and wagging. Tigger would jump from the floor into my arms. Tina, however, would stop a foot or two short of jumping, her head and tail drooping, and wait for me to bend down and stroke her. I think I know why.

One time, and only once, when Tina started to jump into my arms with muddy feet, I snapped her smartly on the nose, and I continued to scold her for a few moments, telling her she was a bad dog! It happened only once but she remembered and was afraid. It takes a lot of stroking to overcome abuse, even mild abuse and, while I learned from Tina never to strike a dog in anger, I had not yet learned the extreme value of positive stroking.

I put it all together one night in a hassle with my five year-old son. He and I belonged to the Y.M.C.A. Indian Guides, an organization that promoted father-son activities such as camping, fishing, etc. At one meeting the fathers decided to have the sons bring a contribution to each meeting, the stipulation being that it must be money they had earned. As we prepared to go to the next month's meeting Douglas asked me for a dime to give as his contribution.

"Did you earn it?" I asked.

"No." he replied.

"Then tonight you simply will not make a contribution. That's the rule!"

"Then I won't go!" he said, and rushed tearfully to his room.

I threatened to paddle him and then I thought of Tina and it occurred to me that there might be a better way to deal with the situation. I knocked on his door and when I finally gained entrance I said, "Son, I was wrong in threatening to spank you. You are a fine young man. I love you very much and I want us to go to the meeting tonight. So how can we handle this problem of you not having earned the dime?"

"If you give me the dime now, I can earn it tomorrow."

I gave him a hug, he took my hand and we went to the meeting and that is how we solved the problem, with love and understanding and respect. That is positive stroking. From the time I became aware of its power to heal I missed few opportunities to stroke Douglas...and my dogs.

When the dog breaks the rule about growling at strangers, it is always wise to give her a firm order that she understands, "Sit!" or "Down!" (Dogs find it difficult to growl and practically impossible to bark when they are lying down and the awareness that they can obey a simple order has a calming effect.) Once they have obeyed that firm but gentle instruction, they deserve an abundance of stroking. Given enough positive show of caring and love, the symptoms resulting from the abusive treatment may gradually fade. They may always be alert to the signals of former maltreatment but they may also put two and two together and find that it comes out four.

The Tellington TTouch is a system used by the originator to treat many illnesses and behavioral aberrations in animals. It consists mainly in touching the animal in a repetition of circles, beginning at 6 as it appears on a clock face and moving slowly around the circle past 6 to 8, then repeating. It appears to calm animals and to improve their health remarkably. I doubt that the circular motion has much to do with the improvement. It seems to me that the value of the TTouch is that someone takes time to physically stroke the animal, thereby conveying a message "I care," and "you are important to me." The attitude of "I care about you," builds confidence and with self-confidence comes gradually a restructuring of self-esteem and a lessening of destructive behavior.

14

About Thrift Of Words

Most of us use too many words in the attempt to say what we mean to say. Often we add unnecessary prepositions to an otherwise complete statement. The old rule for taking showers aboard a naval ship that must conserve water is a case in point.

"Wet down,"

"Soap up,"

"Rinse off,"

This might be reduced to, "Wet, Soap and Rinse" without loss of meaning.

Certainly this becomes apparent in communicating with dogs. I recently saw a cartoon showing a man speaking to his dog.

The man was saying, "Okay Ginger! I've had it! You stay out of the garbage! Understand, Ginger? Stay out of the garbage, or else!"

The dog was hearing, "blah blah GINGER blsh blah blah blah blah blah blah blah GINGER blah blah blah blah blah...."

Simple commands work better with dogs than explanatory phrases. The man would have been better understood if he had just said, "NO, GINGER!" or "OUT, GINGER!" So if we want to train our dogs to sit down, we say, "Sit!" or to lie down, we say, "Down!" To train a dog to walk beside me, I don't say, "Ginger, walk beside me," I say, "Heel!" It is even easier for a dog to obey, "Come!" than "Come here!"

There is something about superfluous words that dilute the meaning of the message; words such as *really, very, actually, hopefully* and *surely.* If I say, "It is windy today," it conveys the fact. If I say, "It is *very* windy today," we may take it to mean that it is windier than windy, but how much windier can it be?" If I say, "I am tired," it conveys a feeling. If I say, "I am *really* tired," it casts a shadow of doubt on whether I am or am not. Aside from the redundancy of the superfluous adverbs, their use makes one wonder whether it is *that* windy, and whether I *am* tired, *(actually* and *really!)* Diluting words create vagueness and lead to a measure of disbelief in the receiver.

Other words that aid in the projection of vagueness are phrases such as the repetitive, *You know* and *Do you follow me?* often used in a message that is filled with generalities rather than specifics. All of these are usually superfluous words, extra words thrown in for emphasis or clarity, and instead of that, they dilute and obscure meaning.

According to the dogs, parsimony promotes clarity! Saying what I want to say in the fewest words possible tends to make it easier to understand me.

Of course, because of their limited human vocabulary, dogs are different from people. With people it is usually more important to hear and transmit messages of feeling than to give commands. Still I listen to my dogs' positive and negative responses and am certain (I almost said, *quite certain)* that thriftiness in my use of words, pays *(off)*.

15

About Conditioning

Since Pavlov demonstrated that he could cause dogs to salivate by ringing a bell, we have known about conditioned responses in animals. I see it in my Golden Retriever, Lacy. When I change into my running shoes, she gets excited. She goes to the top of the stairs, tail held high and wagging enthusiastically. The change of shoes means to her, "going for a walk."

It is said that Sigmund Freud's dog timed his sessions with patients by getting up and stretching at the end of a patient's hour of consultation. Lacey does that, too. How does she know when the fifty-minute hour is over? I used to wonder if she has an internal clock that counts off the minutes so that at the appointed time she awakens from her snooze, stands up and stretches and goes to the door.

By watching her (sometimes more closely than I was watching the client) as the end of the hour approached I discovered that she picks up cues from my behavior. About 48 minutes after the hour, I reach for my account book, pick it up and place it on my side desk. Then I open my appointment book in preparation for scheduling the next session. These are signals to her that the time to break up this meeting is at hand. She opens one eye at the sound of my movement toward these arrangements for closing. Rather than keeping time with her internal clock she has been conditioned over a period of time to respond to my behavior.

So, I have been conditioned by years of getting up at 6:30 each morning, to awaken at about 6:25. By conditioning, I feel a need for my early morning cup of coffee. It is largely conditioning that causes me, without thinking, to turn on the television to the channel 5 news and to do a multitude of tasks, from taking a shower to opening the office in preparation for morning clients.

My conditioning goes further than that in determining my behavior. When I go to the haberdasher I don't consider buying a green tie or a green suit or a green sweater, but instead am attracted to blues and browns. Past experience dictates to me limits on my perimeters of choice. I am limited by conditioning.

Some mornings Lacey doesn't come downstairs to my office with me. Could it be that she sometimes *decides* to stay at the top of the stairway? Sometimes she doesn't respond to my putting on my walking shoes or my suggestion that it is time for a walk. I think that she has taught me one other thing about conditioning. That when circumstances are a bit different, perhaps when a bit of arthritis has invaded her hindquarters, it is OK to decide not to be governed by conditioned response.

More so with me than with my dog conditioning may get in the way of constructive thinking and decisive behavior. It might be better for me to decide to get up at 7:30, not to have coffee each morning and listen to the news, or for that matter, not to take a shower. And come to think about it, I might look very good wearing green!

16

About Patience

If one means by "patience" taking adverse situations calmly then dogs can be great teachers. They bear all sorts of abuse and neglect without a murmur or a protest. My soon to be fourteen-year-old Golden Retriever has developed some arthritis in her hindquarters which she endures without complaint. She still wags her tail when invited to go for a walk and although she walks more slowly and occasionally falters a bit in her movement, seems to enjoy the activity.

When I awaken on a cold winter morning to find six inches of snow on the ground, I feel a bit discouraged at the thought of clearing the walks and the driveway. Then I let my dogs outside and what do they feel? They prance and dance and root their noses in the white stuff as though to say, "Snow is the most wonderful gift that life hands to us!" And after watching them romp for awhile I attack the job of shoveling snow with a different attitude. It is a beautiful thing to see snow covering everything with a mantle of whiteness, and I quite enjoy the task.

Not all of the things my dogs and I are called upon to endure patiently are beautiful. Some are restraining and some are even painful.

At the moment I have a young puppy who loves to romp and play with the older dog, who is not quite up to such rough activity. When Lacey want to go outside, I put Graham on a chain so that she can't infringe on Lacey's privacy. To my astonishment, Graham sits quietly on her chain, only her tail moving in a way that says "It's OK to be chained for awhile."

And there are times when Lacey is obviously hurting from the pain of growing old with its accompanying aches and discomfort. At those time, when I sit by her and stroke her she looks at me with some sadness in her eyes, but her tail still wags in appreciation of my effort to comfort her.

My thoughts go back to a wise gentleman I met in Kyoto, Japan. Mr. Tanaka was the manager of a huge department store who took time out from his busy life to show my family and me the beauty of his ancient city. After visiting a Zen temple in the morning, the afternoon was to be spent touring the Katsuura Imperial Detached Palace. At lunch time a heavy rain began that was to continue all afternoon. When we arrived at the Palace, Mr. Tanaka reached into the trunk of the car and pulled out umbrellas for each of us.

After moving through the superb simplicity of the palace building we raised our umbrellas in preparation for stepping out into the enchanting garden. We moved out into the rain and immediately sought shelter in a covered cloister adjacent to the large pond that was central to the garden. There, protected from the rain, we looked about for our host. At last we found him. He was sitting on a stone bench at the edge of the water, sitting in the rain, his umbrella folded, with a look of serenity on his face that seemed to say, "What a beautiful experience, to see this lovely garden in the rain!"

Mr. Tanaka was a devotee of Zen. And a part of Zen is the art of practicing patience; patience, defined as the acceptance of adverse situations with serenity.

In fact there is an old Japanese saying that speaks to it: "Five pounds of patience are worth a bushel of brains!"

17

About Working, Thinking And Feeling

There is some question about whether dogs have the power of logical thinking. When I throw a ball behind an obstruction, and my dog, after studying the situation for a moment, goes through a door to get to the other side of the obstruction, it appears to me that she has visualized in her mind that it may be possible to get to the ball by going around to the other side. I observe this process in my puppy who likes to chase squirrels. Once the squirrel goes up a tree she loses sight of it until she makes what appears to be a decision to move out a few feet or to go to another side of the tree to get a clearer view.

There is some question about whether dogs work. A seeing-eye dog seems to enjoy guiding his master through a maze of streets. Watching the Alaskan dog sled races I am impressed by the exuberance of the team as it anticipates pulling a heavy sled through the snow. Even the dogs that are trained to sniff out drugs or hunt for survivors in the ruins of an earthquake appear to be playing rather than working. Of course, implied in this question is whether work can be enjoyable and what differentiates work from play.

There is no question that dogs feel. Watch my Golden Retriever put her head between her paws or crawl into her kennel crate when I say, "See you later, Lacey," as I prepare to leave the house without her. Or see the grin that transforms her face with radiance when she welcomes my son returning home after a year's absence. Or notice how she lies down on her side and relaxes with a sigh when I sit down next to her to massage her arthritic hips.

For that matter, there is some question about whether all human beings think. Some people seem to be governed by an automatic internal dialogue repeating the same well-worn phrases over and over so that little, if any, thinking takes place. We often speak of reactive behavior as "thoughtless," meaning it is controlled by impulse or compulsion rather than by thought.

And not all people work. There are those among us who spend their time in leisure activities that require no work-effort.

Dogs may not think and they may not work but I am certain that they feel. Not all people think, not all people work but it is certain that everyone feels.

René Descartes said, "I think, therefore I am!" That became corrupted into, "In order to be worthy, I *have* to think!" The Industrial Revolution paraphrased Descartes: "I work, therefore I am!" That became perverted in the Puritan Movement which, in essence, said, "If I want to be worthy, I *have* to work!" So many of us in this modern age feel counterfeit unless we are great thinkers and hard workers.

The dawning of the Age of Aquarius asserted the final proof of being: "I feel, therefore I am!" And that cannot be prostituted because everybody feels. Not everyone thinks, not everyone works, but everyone feels. And the fact that I feel proves that I am!

My dogs and I go through life believing in our valued existence not so much because we think or because we work. We know we are entitled to our lives because we feel!

18

About Enjoying One's Life-Role

Animals are valuable to human society because of their particular and peculiar talents. Camels can travel through arid zones with a minimal need to replenish their personal water supply. Pigs can find truffles in the forests of France. Canaries react to deadly gases in mines. Horses can carry and pull heavy loads. Dolphins have been used to rescue divers at sea.

Dogs stand apart from other animals in the variety of their talents. There are so many things they can do better than other animals or human beings. Some of them are shepherds, herding sheep and cattle with or without a human presence guiding them. Some are hunters, with amazing powers of scent and are used to guide hunters to game, police officers to smuggled drugs and rescuers to people who have been trapped by earthquakes and landslides. Some can be trained to be the eyes of the blind, guiding them through traffic, around obstacles; or trained to turn switches off and on, pick up dropped objects, even retrieve food from refrigerators for other types of handicapped people.

Now they are being recognized as healers. Both dogs and cats contribute to the health and hopefulness of hospital patients, nursing home residents and to the longevity of elderly people living alone.

The interesting thing that caught my attention is that animals, dogs in particular, who have found their helpful roles in life, enjoy their roles immensely. Shepherding dogs sometimes grow depressed when not allowed to practice their art and are rejuvenated when given work to do. Watch drug-sniffing dogs at a baggage carousel in an air terminal and see how much pleasure their task seems to give them. Most of us have seen dogs at work in the televised accounts of earthquake rescue. Notice how exuberant they are as they search for victims and when they find a living casualty they show unbounded joy.

For several months my teen-age son took our Golden Retriever to a Day Care Center for handicapped people. She would recognize each of the persons present, including the nursing personnel, and let them know that she was available to them. Then she would lie down at my son's feet and look about the group, alert to anyone who might want her to approach. Every aspect of her being expressed her joy at being there and taking part in the activities.

Having earned a Master of Social Work Douglas began his professional career in agencies that minister to the families of teen-agers, those in need of learning how to parent and how to endure parenting. He experimented in several different agencies and left each of them feeling that he was unsuited to the task.

He spent three months in India ministering to outcast lepers. He enjoyed those three months.

Now he is working with homeless people. While the monetary reward is not great, his joy is manifest as he speaks of his work. In a recent letter to me he closed with these words:

> *I had a neat interaction with a homeless man on the street yesterday; I've got a way with people sometimes. It just proves to me that I've got to go with my heart and do the things I believe in with my life.*

He sees himself as an empowerer of the disenfranchised and finds it energizing. He enjoys that role.

People are like dogs that are equipped by temperament and breeding and prepared by training to perform certain tasks. When their roles fit them they enjoy doing whatever they are called upon to do.

19

About Being Tied Up

Just now I have a puppy that is sometimes too active for my older dog so that I have to tie the youngster up when, for example, Lacey wants to have some quiet time to herself in the back yard. I don't like to tie a dog, even though, they accept it gracefully without complaining. It seems cruel to restrain an animal that is so full of happy energy.

Then it occurs to me that my dogs often tie me. They keep me in bondage to them by limiting my coming and going. They are dependent upon me for their food and water, their medications, their trips to the backyard to relieve themselves, and they are dependent upon me to love them and train them so that other people can love them too.

Every year or so I go to Italy to teach psychotherapy. At least a month before I go I begin preparing for their keep. I seek out a kennel that will take good care of them or I arrange for my daughter to look after them with occasional relief by other people who will take them for a weekend. I write out, for the caretakers, instructions about their diets and their exercise periods. The day before I depart I deliver the dogs to their place of temporary abode.

Sometimes they require special care. I take them for daily walks and I watch them carefully for signs of worm and flea infestation. I take them to the Vet at least twice a year for examination.

Right now, the puppy is on some complicated medication, which requires me to give her an antibiotic twice a day, 8:00 in the morning and 5:00 at night. That means I have to juggle my evening engagements so that I can either medicate her an hour early or perhaps two or three hours late. She also requires an oral injection each morning. I feed my dogs twice a day, about 7:00 in the morning and about 3:00 in the afternoon. I may devote more time to my dogs than many dog-owners, but all who own dogs know that their lives are somewhat restricted by their dependency.

Which leads me to an awareness that other things complicate my life, too. In fact every relationship I have entangles me to some degree. So do the things I own, my car for example. It must be serviced regularly, fueled often, washed and waxed occasionally, all of which require my time and energy. So I have come up with a plan to evaluate my dogs, my relationships and my property.

I ask myself two questions:

1) What am I getting out of the relationship? and,
2) What am I giving up in order to maintain it?

Weighing these two questions puts the matter into perspective.

The things I want to get out of my associations are the things I value most: joy, companionship, and dependability. The things I give up in order to maintain the associations are time, energy and money.

What I am giving up in order to have the joy and companionship of my dogs is the freedom to go and come when I please. In other words, my dogs keep me tied, rather tightly, to home.

Each time I tie my puppy up, I am aware that she is tying me, also. When I walk my dog we are both attached to the same leash.

20

About Ways Of Talking

Dr. Karl Menninger used to say that in talking with one another we use subjects and predicates plus a lot of static. He said that if you want to know what is being said, listen to the static.

Dogs do not use subjects and predicates. They speak mostly in the form of verbs and they don't use words to do it. They speak by barking, growling, whining, howling and yelping in various modulations and volumes, each of which have special meanings. They also communicate in other ways: by sense of smell with other dogs, as well as with humans, by their posturing, and by physical contact. There is some indication that there is a mental telepathy by which dogs know what people are planning to do, but I think that this is largely a keen observation of clues.

My dogs have taught me to look for the clues... Lacey has a different bark when she is asking to go outside than she does when she wants a dog biscuit. She has a low-throated "ARGH" when she wants me to play with her. I can tell if she is happy, afraid, content or excited by the way she carries her tail, high and waving for happy, tucked in for afraid, gently fluttering when she is content, whipping back and forth when she is excited. There is a difference between the whimpering of a lonesome puppy and the yapping for food or exercise by a bored puppy. In a dog's facial expression I sometimes see fear or joy and often I see curiosity manifested by a tilt of the head.

What I have learned about listening involves all of my senses: my hearing, for words that clutter the simplicity of a subject and predicate; my eyes, for body language that usually speaks more loudly than the words that are being uttered; my feelings which I find often tell me more about what another person is feeling than he or she has revealed; my sense of smell, in one instance a heavy perfume that indicated a need to cover up something by the person who was speaking; my sense of touch that lets me know by a sweaty palm that the other person is nervous or upset. While I have not yet used the sense of taste in communicating, I reserve the right to do so when the occasion arises.

It has also taught me to watch my own body language. If I am shaking my head negatively while making a positive statement it may be that I am not so confident as I sound. When I notice that I have my arms folded across my chest while listening to a person confiding in me, I know that by unfolding them I will better hear what that person is saying.

Of course I learned much of this in Psychology 101. My dogs have simply reminded me of the fact that communication depends not so much on a subject and a predicate as the static!

21

About Making Mistakes

Human beings make mistakes. The cashier at the supermarket sometimes comes up with a wrong total. Once long ago, my bank made an error in my balance by depositing my check in someone else's account. Occasionally, the postman pushes other people's mail into my mail slot. Automobile repair shops sometimes fix the wrong thing or fail to fix the car's problem. C.P.A.s frequently have to be corrected by the I.R.S. and the I.R.S. people sometimes have to be corrected by an alert C.P.A. Mail Order Houses are famous for sending the wrong size garment, sometimes because shoppers fail to give the correct information. According to Alexander Pope, "To err is human..."

Being human, I make mistakes, lots of mistakes. What have dogs taught me about that?

Dogs make mistakes. I came into the house a few days ago bundled up because the weather was frigid. My puppy had never seen me dressed that way and she growled fiercely at her first sight of me. Even with her keen nose she erred in her identification of me. Sometimes she nips too hard on the older dog and the older dog sharply nips back, saying in effect, you made a mistake that time!

Lacey is an almost perfect dog. She is loving, communicative, adapts immediately to situations. She obeys commands to sit, lie down, heel, knows the word, "No!," doesn't get underfoot, barks quite softly and likes to play.

But she does make mistakes, or what appear to human beings to be mistakes. When she finds some ill-smelling material she may roll in it. She refuses to sleep on her own cushion but likes to steal a nap on a cushion owned by a Border Collie that belongs to my daughter. And once or twice in her fourteen years she has relieved herself on the living room carpet. She also sometimes dribbles a bit of water on the kitchen floor from her water dish. She makes enough mistakes that I can think of her sometimes as almost human.

According to the rest of Pope's statement, "to forgive is divine." When it comes to living with dogs, forgiveness is not just divine, it is imperative. But how can one forgive a repeated mistake or a stain on the living room carpet. Nietzsche said that we can endure almost any *how* if we understand the *why*. This is the key to forgiveness: to understand the *why*. Why do my dogs make mistakes? Because they are afraid, or because it is their nature, or because they forget.

Why do I make mistakes? Usually because I am afraid, or it is my temperament, or I forget. Those are the same reasons parents make mistakes in rearing children. Those are the same reasons everyone makes mistakes in dealing with loved ones and friends and enemies.

Just now the Congress and the President have caused the Federal Government to shut down, by all reasoning a tragic mistake. Why? Because of fears of losing face, or fears of injustice, depending on whose side of the conflict you may be.

If I forgive my dogs for the mistakes they make because I know the *why* of their behaviors, I can forgive the Congress and the President and other people and myself for the myriad of mistakes that are registered in daily living.

I am glad my dogs make a few mistakes. Otherwise how would I know that they, too, are human?

22

About Dignity And Impudence

A friend recently presented me with a print of an oil painting done in the mid 1880s by Sir Edwin Lanseer, a British artist. It shows two dogs. One is a large, staid, long-eared dog, with composure written all over its countenance, hair smooth, eyes mirroring depths of calmness. The other is a small, mischievous wire-haired mutt, with perky ears and eyes that fairly glitter with devilment.

I love that picture. Both animals remind me of dogs I have known. Edwin Lanseer (1802-1873) is famous for his animal paintings. This one is titled: "Dignity and Impudence."

And both remind me of people I know. Some people are dignified, tranquil as deep pools of water. My friend Bob is like that. He just finished a second masters degree at age 80. His letters to me are so beautifully and elegantly written that I sometimes have to force myself to answer them. I feel shallow in my attempts to match his graceful style. Like the large dog, he reflects a majestic bearing that holds him above small ideas and yet is never aloof.

Other people are playful, mischievous and always ready to have fun. Some of them are punsters who can't resist playing with double meanings and witticisms. Sometimes impudent people lack modesty, use sarcasm, are even insolent at times.

This two-fold classification of people can prove useful. Around people who tend toward being dignified I can refrain from too much frivolity. They tire quickly of such light-hearted frolicking. When I am with people who are tuned in to impudence, I can let my hair down and participate in the trivial talk.

My dogs have taught me how to distinguish between the two types. It is something in their mien, in the way they carry themselves, their very posture. It shows in their eyes and in the way they hold their mouths. So I don't joke very much with a sober and formal friend, never with a tight-lipped, serious boss.

My dogs have also taught me not to take the insolence of another person too much to heart. Impudent people, like impudent dogs, are usually not mean...they are just tuned in to another drumbeat. While impudence, in the form of sarcasm or insolence, is a form of hostility, it is not necessarily aimed at the person receiving it. It may be a brassy reaction to a world that is seen as unfair, or it may be simply a counter-reaction to a sense of low self-esteem.

One thing seems certain: dignity reflects a self-assurance and a sense of security, while impudence mirrors a constant awareness of threat. When a puppy is playful, it sometimes nips or growls or barks which appear to be protective behaviors devised to counter threat.

Both dignity and impudence make for attractive people as well as interesting dogs. They represent two sides of a world, which I must take seriously even while I laugh at its peculiarities and imperfections.

23

About Noise

The beautiful puppy I got from the pound had been the victim of abuse and/or neglect and as a result she had lots of fears. She was particularly afraid of noises.

Lawn mowers are noisy. On any summer afternoon from my backyard I can hear one or more of them cutting the grass on a neighbor's lawn. So are leaf-blowers and (I live in a woods), chain saws. Airplanes roar overhead and on a clear crisp night I can hear trains whistle from a mile or more away. Doorbells are noisy as are timers and even striking clocks. Occasionally neighbors have a party at a swimming pool or in the back garden and they bring out the boom boxes with the latest hard-rock music blaring into the night.

I was not aware of how noisy the world is until I began my daily walks with Graham. Children are noisy. In their play they utter short, startling, staccato shouts as when they are playing football someone yells out, "CATCH IT!" It is the more startling because, for the passer-by, whether it be dog or human, it shatters the silence unexpectedly.

What brought this to my attention was the dog's reaction to the noise of suddenly accelerating cars. I had never noticed that cars make a rather eerie swooshing kind of noise when they start to move or begin to speed up while moving. The sound of it was scary to Graham. A car could pass us on the street and she would pay no attention to it, but the moment the driver stepped on the gas pedal, there came that sound of SWIIISSH and Graham would start and move away from the noise and toward me.

It occurs to me that Graham is expressing overtly what most people feel sub-consciously. We have grown so used to noise that we hardly pay any outward attention to the constant din of our existence. But perhaps we pay a price in terms of wear and tear on our nervous system. I once had an office directly under the final approach to Lindbergh field in downtown San Diego. Planes landing every few, minutes would drown out any conversation taking place in that office. For a few weeks it bothered me terribly. Like Graham I wanted to get away from it. When a plane came overhead I would look up and follow its movement with my ears and my eyes. But after awhile I responded differently. If I were talking I would stop for a few seconds until the noise reduction allowed me to be heard. And this was automatic. That is to say, I was not even aware that a plane was passing overhead. I automatically allowed for its passage by stopping talking.

Then I moved to suburban Maryland, a place where noises are abundant but where only occasionally do I hear the roar of a distant plane. It seemed to me that my nervous system relaxed a bit as it grew accustomed to many sounds but of a more tranquil nature.

It also comes to me that I have been part of the problem of noise pollution. Perhaps not outside of my own home. I do not yell, I keep my lawnmower and car mufflers in good condition. I don't operate outdoor power equipment during the hours when neighbors are sleeping. But inside my home, where my friends and I (and my dogs) are the only victims, I have become aware that the stereo and TV don't need to be turned up so high and instead of yelling to a person in another room, I can go where she is and speak to her in a quieter voice.

This is not only beneficial to others it is good for me, too. I feel more relaxed when I maintain a quiet atmosphere in my home. And my dogs have taught me something else. As a rule they respond more favorably to a quiet command than they do to a shouted command. One of the things I've learned about all of this is condensed in the very words I say to my dogs when they are barking. Softly, I say, "Let's keep it quiet!"

24

About A Different Perspective

Pussy cat, pussy cat, where have you been?
I've been to London to see the queen.
Pussy cat, pussy cat, what did you there?
I frightened a little mouse, under her chair!
— *Nursery Rhyme*

It is impossible to understand a dog so long as your mind remains in a standing position. That's because dogs go on all fours and perceive most of their world (the part that's controlled by human beings at least) from below. Imagine yourself confined to the lower two and one-half feet of the five or six feet you now occupy. Think of how people would appear large and looming over you. Think of how huge and noisy a car would seem to be. The chances are you would tend to be either submissive or rebellious in such an overwhelming atmosphere.

I sometimes get down on my hands and knees to observe the world of my home from a dog's perspective. Tables and chairs look different from down there. It is difficult to see out of windows. I can't reach the tops of kitchen counters. And people seem to be made up mostly of feet and legs.

The truth about it is, Dogs are not human! They are different from human beings in several ways. For one thing, they have highly developed senses of hearing and smelling. It is reported that a dog's olfactory ability is 1,000 times that of the average human being. That, in itself, would lend a different perspective to the way he sees his world. Imagine relying more on one's sense of smell than on one's vision. A garbage container would contain a storehouse of information instead of just being an unsightly object. Imagine the alertness that would come from hearing approaching steps to your front door when you are in the upstairs back bedroom!

The old Indian thought about not judging another person until you have walked a mile in his moccasins occurs to me when I think of how different my dog is from me. I anthropomorphize and attribute to her many of the qualities that I possess. I say she is jealous, but it would be more correct to say that, by instinct, she is being protective of her territory. I think, sometimes, that she is being stubborn, failing to see that what is important to her is different from what is important to me. A mouse may be more important than a queen!

In the same way I tend to judge other people by my own standards. I notice this particularly in the realm of what people wear. I am conservative in dress, wear lots of drab, earth colors and I have an underlying belief that the proper way to dress is just that. I go in for basic black and pearls! Afro-Americans have a different set of values. They like color. Black women often wear flowing garments with lots of reds and purples and oranges and yellows.

Although I am becoming used to it, I am still a little shocked to see the Mayor of Washington D.C. wearing colorful headbands and kente cloths. As an experiment, I try walking in his moccasins for a day. I wear an orange striped shirt with a bright purple sweater and, to my surprise, get compliments. By the end of the day I find myself liking the added colors.

In the same way, although I may not actually practice some of the extreme behaviors I see in others, I can imagine myself living that way. I wear a pair of mental moccasins for a few minutes and visualize myself going to a nightclub with deafening rock and roll music splitting the air. I can only stand a few minutes of such daydreaming, but in those moments I gain a new perspective on what other people enjoy.

If I went to London to see the queen I would not be distracted by lesser things such as tabloid pictures of Princess Di in her exercise salon. But give me time and I may come to it!

25

About Sexuality

I think there is a striking similarity between dogs and people when it comes to the expression of sexual desires and behavior. For one thing, the male dog is the pursuer. Sex seems to be more important to him than anything else and certainly more important to him than it is to the female dog.

A big black Labrador Retriever named Barney serves as a model. Whenever a female dog was present Barney became the aggressive pursuer. The female, on the other hand, appeared coy and reluctant. She would move away from Barney, tail tucked between her legs. After several minutes of this ritualistic dance, Barney would give up and stop the active pursuit. At which point the female dog would approach in a kind of hesitant and inquiring manner and the charade would begin again until, at last the consummation of the act.

In our stereotyping, at least, this is a parody of human behavior. This holds that men are more interested in sex than are women; that men tend constantly to aspire to sexual conquest; while women, though interested in the matter, tend to be coquettish and demure. While the raping of women by men is all too commonplace, the raping of men by women is almost never headlined. So our stereotyping portrays men as the aggressors and women as the more reluctant receptors.

The covers' of women's magazines such as Cosmopolitan tend to belie this stereotyping. Listed in bold-type are the titles of articles that lead one to believe that female sexual desire and female sexual performance are the paramount topics of discussion. Perusing these articles, however, casts a different perspective on human female behavior. Like the female dog, the female of the human race is not to be too demanding; rather her expressions of desire are couched in subtleties: enticement, romantic settings, and flirtatious behavior. She is advised on what to wear, how to scent herself, how to be suggestive in her approach to her desired male. Not to be too flagrant in her behavior, lest she frighten the suitor away.

Let's face it! Male and female dogs are both interested in sex! So are both men and women, although women were more nervous about such things as pregnancy until we got the pill and more skittish about their reputations and more restricted by parental admonition than were men.

Added to this is the extreme passivity of most men. In thirty-five years of counseling I have found that most seductions are arranged by the woman rather than by the man. Men are more passive than women. They wait for the invitation of the woman. Even the aggression called rape is passive-aggressivity. Women are more decisive than men and most of the seductions they initiate are the result of decisions.

Which brings us back to dogs. The male dog doesn't decide to have sex. He impulsively and passively-aggressively attempts the conquest. On the other hand, I think I perceive in the female dog's retreat and final advances, a decision to go through with the experience, be it enjoyable or disagreeable.

26

About Aggressivity

Our big Black Labrador was a male and watching him I came to realize how much like a male human being he was. Our Golden Retriever is a female and observing her I think I see in her the same qualities as the human female.

First off, Barney was competitive. He urinated frequently, not to empty his bladder but to stake out his territory. He barked furiously at other male dogs, although up close he was as friendly as an old shirt. Unless there was a female close by. Then the hair on the back of his neck would stand up and he would assume a defensive stance. And whenever there was a female dog present, you could expect Barney to respond with an erection.

Second, Barney was muscular and strong. He seldom got tired, and when he did get tired he stretched out and slept with one-eye open, responding in a flash to any would-be intruder of his territory.

Lacey, on the other hand, seemed to be more at home with company. While she, too, covers any urination spots of another female with her own, it seems more like an act of protection of her territory than a defense of it. She loves other dogs of both sexes and when she encounters an aggressive animal she lowers her tail and turns away rather than defends her space. Of course it would be different if she had puppies. From past experiences with mother dogs and their litters, I know how protective the maternal instinct can be. Still it seems just that, protective, rather than defensive.

What is the difference in the male and the female dog? According to recent studies we might think of the difference in the way the two hemispheres of the brain are connected, the male being more spatially oriented and operating from one hemisphere and the female more relationship oriented using both sides of the brain.

But with dogs, and perhaps with men, I consider most of the difference to be between the hormone testosterone and the hormone estrogen. There is something about testosterone that promotes aggresivity. Most wars are sanctioned and fought by men. They march off aggressively to do battle. Men are defenders of what they conceive of as their own space. I assume that there is something about testosterone that promotes defensiveness. Women are protectors of the family and the community, so I assume there is something about estrogen that promotes relationships.

At least I have become aware of the difference in the male and the female psyches. Whether due to hormonal secretions, training or a collective unconscious, males tend to be competitive, women tend to think in terms of relationships. When a male driver approaches the entrance ramp to a freeway, usually he is spatially interpreting how he can move ahead of the next car in the flow of traffic. When a woman approaches the entrance ramp she usually is thinking of how she relates to the other cars and their drivers. Men tend to think their way into the traffic flow. Women tend to feel their way into the traffic flow.

While I don't think it possible to change the competitive nature of men in one or two generations, I should like to see women more involved in governing our communities and our nations. If it is true that women comprise more than 50% of our population, let that be the ratio of men-to-women in congress, in governmental agencies, on school boards and city and county councils. Once the ratio tips in favor of women, the result might be spectacular. For one thing the defensive-competitive nature that women are forced to exhibit as a minority in governmental functions would disappear and the emphasis on relationships would grow. For another, the present emphasis on defensive armament would no doubt be drastically lessened.

Men have been in control of our world long enough to prove that they do a pretty imperfect job of governing. Perhaps the hope of the world is that sometime, women will bring to bear their influence on nations and their influence of human values.

27

About Praise And Punishment

The difference in praise and punishment as a corrective procedure is well known, particularly among elementary school teachers. Punishment tends to defeat correction. It says, in effect, "You are not OK." It punches down one's feeling of self-worth, and lowers self-esteem. Punishment is the negative approach to correcting behavior. It places minus signs on the closed eyelids and invites us either to feel guilty and submit or to feel defiant and rebel.

Still punishment has its place. Probably the most corrective form of punishment is that which is a direct result of an unwanted behavior as when a child touches a hot stove and receives a minor burn. The child will probably not touch that hot stove again. The values of direct result punishment are 1) that it is immediate, thus forming an indelible link between the behavior and the consequence and 2) the obvious lesson in natural relationship: “the punishment fits the crime.”

These two features, immediacy and associated consequence, are not always easy to maintain as, for example, when a child turns a fish bowl over spilling the fishes onto the carpet. The related consequence would seem to be immediately to have the child rescue the fish, refill the bowl with de-chlorinated water and place it back where it belongs after mopping up the spilled water. But here one must consider the quick mortality of fish on a dry carpet plus the lack of personal consequences to the child. It might be an opportunity, without punishing, after cleaning up the mess and restoring the proper orientation for the fish, to sit down with the child on the lap and explain to him about the importance of keeping hands off the fish bowl. An alternative would be an immediate soft swat on the child's behind, accompanied by a word of explanation.

Nowhere is the association between punishment and praise and behavior more apparent than in the training of dogs. I have learned from my dogs that punishment, unless it is immediate, is not corrective. Rather, it is demeaning and counter-productive. An exuberant puppy naturally wants to jump up on people. A quick way to change that behavior is to catch the puppy's front feet, and step gently on her rear feet. Usually, after one or two repetitions, she will get the message. Like a baby, a puppy explores the world with her mouth. When she bites my hand I immediately grasp her muzzle and hold her mouth tightly shut for a few seconds. In teaching her to heel, I use a choke-chain, which immediately closes down when she pulls too far ahead. In these corrective measures the consequences are immediate and related to her behavior. It is what I refer to as *being faced with reality*. After each of these corrections I praise her, saying, "What a good dog!" and occasionally give her a small treat.

Dogs, like children, love to be praised. And at the first, like children, they want to please the people who care for them. When you praise a puppy or a child you are saying, "You are OK!" and building a sense of self-worth and self-esteem.

I try not to make the mistake of phony praise. I don't say, "My, what a good dog!" until after she has stopped jumping, biting or pulling. Only as soon as the correction has taken place, comes the time for praise and, like punishment, it should be immediate.

Not only puppies and children, adults too, respond negatively to punishment and positively to praise when it is sincere. Try it on your husband, wife, brother, sister, aunt, uncle, boss and co-worker. Look for their finer qualities and when you see one, mention it. An excellent form for doing that is, "I like the way you (dress, keep your desk neat, stay with a job until it is completed, smile, are friendly, etc.) Then notice how they respond in a positive way.

In fact both puppies and children, as well as adults, would not turn over nearly so many fishbowls if, from their earliest days, they were stroked for their gracefulness, their care of property, their attentiveness and their friendliness.

28

About Random Behavior

Some time ago, I learned that dogs are creatures of habit. So, when I take my dogs for a walk they always turn to cross the street at the same place, they almost always urinate and defecate in the same general area of the back yard. They wake up at precisely seven o'clock every day and they bark to alert me that it's time for a milk bone at 11:00 each morning.

Training is based on consistent, positive stroking and a treat received when they conform to the instructions. It is easy to train a dog to sit by giving the command, "sit" and each time the dog obeys, giving her a treat and lavish praise. The key is consistency.

When I trained my Golden Retriever to go to the same spot, in the furthest reaches of the backyard, to defecate, she followed the maxim that dogs are creatures of habit. When, however, I got my new 8-week-old mixed Briard and faithfully led her to the same spot for two weeks without a failure, then turned her loose, where did she go? She went immediately to the side yard where she continues to go, usually, until this day. And now, the Golden has followed her leading and sometimes fails to follow her earlier training.

And just sometimes when I ask a well-trained dog to "sit," the dog will look at me with bewilderment cocking her head from side to side as if to ask what it is I want her to do.

Random behaviorisms are as much a part of a dog's life as a human being's. I too, am a creature of habit. I wake up at 6:30 every morning, stumble in and out of the bathroom, enter my kitchen and start the water heating for oatmeal and coffee and flip on the TV to hear the morning news. That is I usually do things in that order. But sometimes, I change the routine out of an impulse to have bran flakes instead of oatmeal, and to listen to classical music instead of watching the news.

Furthermore, like my dogs, I am usually even-tempered and not given to criticism. So I am a bit surprised when one of my dogs acts as though she does not hear a command or when I find myself bitching about someone's behavior or something misplaced. So I have learned to accept randomness as well as consistency in my own life and in the lives of other people.

And if someone says to me, "You are being inconsistent!" I shall reply, "Very well, I am not always consistent!"

29

About Seeing Other Dogs

All of the books on dog training remind me to remember that my dogs think of me as another dog. A lot of the success of training depends on whether they see me as a superior dog or a subordinate dog. If they see me as top-dog, they will tend to obey my commands, come when they are called and want to be with me. If they see me as an underdog they will be less responsive to my controls and may ignore my overtures. In all of our interactions they will deal with me as though I were another dog.

An old Russian proverb says that if an ox thinks of God, he thinks of him as a bigger ox. That may explain why when children try to conceptualize God they imagine him as a male parent or as an old man with a beard. It also may explain something of the way human beings see other human beings: that is, we tend to think of other people as having the same thoughts, feelings and behavior that we have, and we can't imagine why everyone hasn't done as we would have done in a given situation. In other words, we tend to think of other people as "other dogs."

As a psychotherapist I am often confronted with a person's behavior which is obviously (to me) self-destructive. Why does a person repeat old behavior patterns that precipitate trouble for himself and others? Why, for example, does a woman who divorces one wife-beater select another abusive male as her next spouse? I wouldn't do that. In order to be of help I must see that person as different from me.

I dislike cluttered kitchens. I can tolerate some stains on my countertops so long as they are kept free of unnecessary things. My friend, on the other hand, doesn't seem to mind clutter but is a fiend for cleanliness. We clash because neither of us considers that we are people with different experiences in our backgrounds who feel and react differently to stimuli such as clutter and cleanliness.

Then too, like dogs, we tend to think in terms of a hierarchy of importance and power. In psychological terms this is known as transference and counter-transference. We put people in power categories. Some people we see as authority figures and others we see as secondary to ourselves and treat them accordingly.

I take a reverse lesson from my dogs. I understand (usually) that they are dogs, more interested in food than I am. More interested in chasing squirrels than I am. More creatures of conditioning than I am.

And I apply that lesson to my friends and loved ones. They are not made in my exact image. They are different from me in the ways they think and feel and act.

The lesson is that there is no one else in the world exactly like me. So, if I tend to think of people as "other dogs" I need to consider, at least, that there are many different breeds of dogs with different characteristics. So I will not expect a Chow-chow to think and act like a Golden Retriever!

30

About Mixing Breeds

Run down a list of the problems affecting purebred dogs and you will find a lot of afflictions that plague inbreeding of blood lines. In the creation of distinct breeds we have accidentally concentrated detrimental genes resulting in a high potential for inherited diseases and malformations. The Doberman is noted for a high rate of heart disease, the retrievers and other large breeds for an increased risk, of hip dysplasia. Skin allergies and nervous temperaments are only two of many manifestations of problems in purebred dogs.

Mixed breeds, by the very randomness of their breeding, are less likely to fall victim to inherited disorders. And in my experience with dogs mixed-breed dogs, with their mixed colors and hair formations, are almost always strangely beautiful!

Health and beauty! Both seem enhanced by a mixture of ancestry. If that is true for dogs, then it starts me wondering if we haven't missed the boat by not encouraging inter-national marriages. There are certain superiority's found in all ethnic groups. The black culture seems highly productive of both athletic and musical abilities. The Asian block produces hard-working, intelligent people. The French excel in cuisine. The Germanic peoples are industrious. The Italians are romantic. The British, honor and duty bound, etc.

And as far as the enhancement of beauty goes any visitor to Hawaii or Vietnam will note that a diversity of racial heritage seems to produce an exceptionally attractive person.

Of course, those who acquire young mixed-breed dogs, have less grounds for predicting what their dog will be like and how he/she will fit into their own lifestyle.

In the human realm, however, that is true not only of mixed-races but also of people of similar backgrounds. Consider the plight of royal marriages! No mixture of ethos there and yet the lifestyles and preferences seem to diverge precipitously.

So my association with dogs tempts me to suggest to anyone wanting to acquire a dog: "The advantages of selecting a purebred animal are obvious. You can choose between different temperaments and physical characteristics, thus predicting a breed most suitable to your wishes. But consider the possibility of a random-bred dog, probably more healthy and possibly as beautiful as his pure-bred cousin."

And that same association tempts me to suggest to hide-bound white and black and yellow citizens, "Lets shake up the mixture a bit, perhaps not so much with inter-marriage but more fundamentally in our day-to-day relationships. Let's invite representatives of diverse cultures into our homes, eat with them, play with them, work with them, share with them."

In doing that we may be in for some surprises because different tribes have different conventions and different customs. So, we can learn from the shocks and astonishment and perhaps be enriched by the surprises.

One other considerations of mixed breeds. While there is a demand for the selectively-bred, whether it be in people or in dogs, it is the randomly bred people and dogs that are often most in need of good relationships and good homes!

31

About If It Runs, Chase It!

I have just finished reading a newspaper item about a child that was attacked by a Pit Bull Dog. The item noted that when the dog approached her, the little girl was frightened and began to run. It struck me that that is usually the case. When something or someone runs, the dog gives chase and some dogs attack. If the child had stood still, the dog probably would not have been so aggressive. Still, it's as natural to run when you are afraid as it is for the dog to chase whatever runs.

I have noticed that about most of my dogs. They may live in peace with the house cats who pay them little attention or even make a stand, back arched and hissing at their approach. Most of my dogs have gotten along well with the cats I have owned as well as the neighborhood cats, which remain unmoved by familiar dogs. On walks my dogs ignore the motionless cat sitting by the stoop or in the driveway of a home.

It is when the cat moves that the dog becomes alert and when the cat runs away the dog wants to give chase.

This fact is used in the training of dogs to come on command. When you have a dog who pays no attention to the word, "come," or a whistle or a gesture, usually, it will follow you if you rapidly walk away.

One of the most painful situations in life is to lose a love-object to someone else or to something other than death. Every psychotherapist knows that the best advice she can give to one who has suffered rejection is to non-attach, to recognize that it is important to get on with ones s own life rather than pursue the love object that has run away. If you give chase, the other person tends to move further away. If, on the other hand, you move away and begin to build new relationships the other person will often return to pursue you.

There is a second lesson to be learned from this concept: when you run away from a frightening situation instead of facing up to it, the fear will become even more haunting. It was Sophocles who said, "To him who is in fear everything rustles." The man who is afraid of becoming ill, discovers aches and pains in abundance.

I used to be afraid of the Internal Revenue Service. I was afraid I would make a mistake on my return, fail to include some remote income or not be able to back up some unusual deduction. Of course, at the same time, I was afraid that I was missing some legitimate deductions that I should be taking. When I received correspondence from the I.R.S. I would be alarmed that it heralded an audit. In a sense I was on the run from the I.R.S. and I felt pursued.

Then I decided to face the matter squarely. I consulted a competent tax-lawyer who looked over my income and deductions and assured me that, while I would probably make some mistakes in the complicated forms of the Internal Revenue Service, I was in fact keeping excellent records and, above all, I would not be going to prison! Thus ended my running and thus ended the chase.

"If it runs, chase it," seems to be a natural phenomena that occurs not only in the life of a dog but perhaps even more often in human experience. So I will stand my ground and if I get bitten at least it will not be because I ran!

32

About Unconditional Love

Most of us think of dogs loving their master unconditionally. We sometimes leave them alone in a house or apartment, or even tied in the back yard, all day and when we come home in the evening they are there to greet us, tails wagging, wanting to show us they love us.

Even mistreated and abused dogs seem to show this kind of affection for the person who feeds them and is responsible for them.

I wonder if it is unconditional love that motivates them. Perhaps it is dependency. The dog depends on its owner for necessities: food, water and exercise. Maybe the dog recognizes that it is a fundamental of survival to show appreciation for its sponsor. Maybe its love is a need kind of love.

How is dependency related to unconditional love? It may seem unromantic to pose that question. All of us want to be loved unconditionally. That is, to be loved not for what we do but for who we are. So a compliment that is applied to us because we have accomplished something worthwhile invites us to feel good about ourselves. But a stroke for being, unrelated to any specific behavior, has a more profound effect on our feeling of self-worth.

"That is a beautiful tie," enables me to feel good about my decision to buy it or to wear it. It is conditional, i.e., it depends on my ability to know the difference between what is pretty and what is not. "You are a beautiful person," allows me to feel good about my being. It is considered to be an unconditional compliment but it, too, has a dependent quality. In effect it says, "So long as you maintain your present state of being, you will be appreciated."

Dependency has two sides. One of them relates to a need on the part of the dog or the person providing the love. The person who gives us the unconditional stroke is not completely altruistic. It enables him to survive or to feel good about inviting me to feel good! Thus, he is dependent. And the person receiving the stroke may feel his worthiness depends on maintaining the state of being that prompted the giver to give it!

Nevertheless there is usually a magical quality to unconditional love, love that is manifested toward us not for something we have done but given to us because of who we are. That's the way dogs love us. After all the arguments of dependency are exhausted, I return home to find my faithful friend looking at me adoringly, (even jumping up on me at times) not because I have left her alone for ten hours but in spite of that fact, because she is glad to see me.

It restores my faith in her, and in dogs in general, and in people, and in life. Somebody believes in me. Somebody loves me for who I am!

33

About Internal Dialogue

Dogs don't argue with themselves. They go about their lives untroubled by doubts and internal arguments. My dogs don't have an internal dispute about their diet. They don't discuss within whether it is fattening or unhealthy, they just eat the food that's put before them or walk away from it. Nor do they question whether they should lie down and sleep or follow me as I go about the house. Their minds are uncomplicated by the rights and wrongs that forest my conscious and unconscious thought processes.

I, as other people, am constantly involved in an internal dialogue. Often it has a moral facet. Should

I omit a cash-payment or include it in my statement of income for the l.R.S? Should I lie to the persistent person on the telephone, by saying, "There s someone at the door, I have to go now," or should I just, say, "I'm going to hang up now?"

Sometimes it is a question concerning my health. I would like to eat the fat part of the steak and I know I shouldn't.

Or a matter of self-confidence. I know I can drive across the water hazard from the 12th tee BUT I exchange an old, beaten up ball for the new one, just in case!

Dogs don't have a sense of right and wrong, of good and evil. They don't worry about what they did this morning minutes or hours or days after they did it. They don't have a conscience. They are not troubled by guilt for past behavior or anxiety about the future. They accept themselves the way they are.

I have a conscience. It is faulty, of course, because it consists of all of the cautions and shoulds that my parent figures instilled in me from the time I was born. Some of the internal messages make sense to me: don't over-eat, get enough sleep, finish the job, be thoughtful of others, clean up your own messes. Some I don't quite know whether to believe or not: anything worth doing is worth doing well, don't show your feelings, etc.!

Others seem to complicate my life, particularly the ones that carry an exaggerated time frame of absolutes: *always* clean your plate, *don't ever* talk too much, *never* tell a lie, *always* be kind and generous, *never* use profanity, *never* give up.

I think it was Ogden Nash who penned these lines:

There's only one way to achieve happiness
On this terrestrial ball;
And that is to have, either a clear conscience,
Or none at all!

Well I have a conscience and my dogs do not. And it is not always clear. It is often confused. So what can I learn from my dogs? Acceptance! Acceptance of myself, particularly my feelings. It's okay to feel anything I feel, including my confusion that is caused by internal dialogue: the "shoulds" and the "should nots," the "I can do it" and the fears that "I cannot do it."

With acceptance there comes a new willingness to trust my own judgment and the resolve *never, never, never* to get caught up in absolutes!

34

About Too Many Treats

Everyone who has trained a dog knows the value of rewards to reinforce desired behavior. This can come in the form of lavish praise, stroking and saying, "What a g-o-o-d dog," and it can come in the form of bite-sized treats. Of the two the latter is probably quicker in establishing obedience but if it is used indiscriminately it runs the risk of being accepted as a right rather than a reward and thus loses its reinforcing effect.

Lavish praise for being a good dog cannot be overdone. Dogs need to feel secure in their relationship to their owners and the more love one gives them the more secure they become. You don't spoil a dog by giving her lots of love. You spoil her by not demanding that she be responsible in her behavior. One way irresponsibility can be developed is by the frequent and wholesale distribution of treats, which the dog comes to take for granted.

It seems to me it is the same way with children. Many of the problem kids I see have developed serious behavior problems because of over-indulgent parents. This may be particularly true in affluent families where money is no problem and children get whatever they want whenever they want it and are not allowed to take responsibility for themselves or their behavior. That kind of leniency can lead a child to demand his or her "rights" in such things as eating what they want to eat, going where they want to go, going with whomever they want to go with and staying out until they want to come home. Like a puppy they are living on a "pleasure-principle" level rather than a "reality-principle" level.

As you would with a puppy you can allow the child to take appropriate responsibility for his age and development level. For the puppy you immediately put him outside when he has an accident on 'the living room rug. For the child you expect him to tie his own shoes by the time he is two years old, pick up his toys at an early age and eat what is served at daily meals. You don't punish the puppy or the child for what he does or does not do. You simply withhold the treats for the dog and for the child, perhaps you curtail his television watching, or his choice of toys or his desert.

You can't love a puppy or a child too much. It's okay to hug your dog and speak softly and lovingly to him as much and as often as you wish.

But treats are for a time when he is exhibiting desired behavior. You don't spoil a child by loving her too much. Spoiled children are children who have not been allowed to take responsibility for their own appropriate development-level behavior.

Loving, while demanding that the one being loved be responsible for himself and his own behavior, and not punishment but reward is the fast track to responsible behavior. What a g-o-o-d puppy! What a g-o-o-d child!

35

About It Always Stops Raining Long Enough To Milk The Cows

My father was a Baptist Minister who liked milk and believed that the best milk came from Jersey cows. He always had one or two Jerseys, or maybe four, and they were kept in a barn and pasture about six blocks from our home in a small Missouri town. In the Spring of the year it often rained a lot and I used to worry about my father having to walk in the rain to care for his cows. His response to my anxiety was, "It always stops raining long enough to milk the cows." To my childhood amazement that always seemed to be true.

I get my milk from cartons purchased at the grocery store so I don't keep any cows. But I do have dogs and I believe that every dog should have a long walk every day. Through the years I have affirmed that what my father said about milking cows also applies to walking dogs. It always stops raining long enough to walk the dogs!

Studying Transactional Analysis with Eric Berne in the sixties I learned about finding a place to park. It was Berne's belief that if you know you are okay you can "always" find a place to park.

It seems to me that the common thread linking these two concepts is a consistent optimism that remains prevalent in one's psyche even when, occasionally, it may rain while milking or walking the dog or all the parking spaces may be filled. It is an optimism that opens an alert awareness in the human mind to see the cessation of rain when it occurs and to notice the empty parking space when it is there. Notice the effect of such optimism.

Optimism opens the awareness by shutting down the internal dialogue that closes it. When we are so concerned about the rain that we keep telling ourselves, "it will never stop," we fail to notice that it has stopped. When we are so pessimistic about finding a parking space that we keep the internal message alive,

"I can never find a parking space," We drive by the available spaces without noticing them.

Optimism is eternally tied to one's own self-esteem. That's where the concept of okay-ness comes in, There's something about dreading walking in the rain that tends to make us believe that it is our fault that it is raining. There's something about not finding a place to park that tells us that we are not okay.

Try this experiment, toss a coin in the air and catch it on your wrist. Say to yourself, "If it comes up heads it means that I'm okay. If it comes up tails it means that I am not okay." Now, without looking at the coin consider your feelings about the anticipated result. Is there even a small part of you that is hoping the coin comes up heads? Such small and completely irrelevant thoughts can tell you something about how easy it is to discount your self-esteem.

One way to improve your self-esteem is to practice optimism. Even superficial optimism is better than superficial pessimism. The next time it is raining and you have to do an errand sometime during the day, say to yourself, "It always stops raining long enough to...." The next time you are driving to a crowded destination say to yourself, "There will be a place to park within a close distance to where I am going."

We give ourselves hundreds of internal messages every day. It can make all the difference in the world when you substitute positive messages for the negative ones.

You may soon find that there is truth in my father's words, "It always stops raining long enough to milk the cows!"

36

About Dysfunctional Families

My dog, Graham, came from a dysfunctional family! Not that her own mother and father were dysfunctional as a dog family. They ate and slept and followed the rituals of most dog families. The father copulated, then went his own way as most dogs do. The mother took over at birth and licked her puppies dry and nudged them up to her teats as most bitches do.

The dysfunctional family she came from was the family who owned her mother. And they were dysfunctional for a justifiable cause. They had to move just as the puppies were born, so they gave them away prematurely. Graham was born the week following Christmas of 1994. She was given away on the 14th of February 1995 at the age of less than eight Weeks. Most authorities agree that it is important for puppies to stay in the litter with their mother until they are at least eight weeks old. It is a time when they are becoming socialized to other dogs, learning how to play within the security of their mother's surveillance.

There is a lot being said these days about dysfunctional families. A whole movement has come forward called, ACOAP, Adult Children of Alcoholic Parents, saying that all families with an alcoholic abuser are dysfunctional. So they are, to a degree. But so are all families more or less dysfunctional.

What is the earmark of a dysfunctional family? Abusive behavior, physical, emotional or verbal. While most families do not abuse their children physically, most families do abuse their own and other children emotionally. It is called discounting and it occurs when a person fails to take into account what another person is feeling, or thinking or doing. This leads the under-valued person to lower his own self-esteem: what I am thinking or feeling or doing, is not important, so I am not important.

Discounting tends to lead to crazy behavior. That is what happened to Graham. At a time when she needed the companionship of her siblings and the protective care of her mother she was treated as though these needs did not really matter. She came to me when she was five months old and It took months of nurturing and gradual socialization with the world out there for her to gain a foothold on her own self-esteem so that she doesn't growl or bark or shy away from other dogs and people. Truly crazy behavior!

The solution to Graham's problem is the same as the solution to the problems of human beings who have been discounted. Letting them know through words and behavior that they deserve to be treated well.

The greater the discounting has been, the more tender loving care it takes to renovate the spirit of those who hold a low self-image. The way to do that with dogs is to praise them lavishly. The way to do it with human beings is to stroke them with sincere, unconditional caring.

And it does not always work! Some people and some dogs have been physically and emotionally abused so severely that they must be cloistered away from society. The number of dogs who, because of crazy behavior, are put down every year, is a graphic reminder that, in human relationships, it is important to take seriously what every individual person thinks, and feels, and does.

37

About Eating Grass

No one has ever explained to me why dogs eat grass. It probably has to do with the regulation of their digestive system. I watch my dogs carefully and in the winter when there is no grass available they don't seem to change their excretory functions nor do they seem any less healthy than in the spring and summer when they seem to crave a daily ration of grass.

For that matter, no one has ever explained to me why dogs turn around three or more times before they lie down. Some say it is dates back to the wilds when they had to push down the high growth before they could be comfortable. Others say they are checking the wind-direction so that they can detect approaching danger. One of the problems with these explanations is that I note that dogs engage in similar behavior before they defecate.

Much of animal behavior is classified as instinctive, arising spontaneously and independent of volition or choice. Birds engage in nest-building, each kind according to an inner template following a pattern apparently established in their DNA.

Most of the automatic behavior of people comes from early instructions. Looking to the left first before crossing the street, putting the hand over the mouth when coughing, rising from a chair to greet a new dinner guest. What about instinctive behavior. Is that part of human function?

Neuro-Linguistic-Programming (NLP) provides some insight into human instinctive behavior in its definition of eye-movement patterns. It observes six distinctive eye-movements used in accessing mental information when we are thinking and feeling. Usually they follow these patterns:

- up and to the Left: visual memories
- up and to the Right: visual constructed images
- on the level Left: remembered sounds
- on the level Right: constructing what to say and how to say it.

- down and to the Left: talking to oneself
- down and to the Right: accessing feelings

While individuals differ in which direction their eyes move when, for example, they are remembering a past event, each person is consistent in the direction of eye movement when he does it as he is also when imagining some future event or accessing a past feeling or predicting a future feeling. Psychotherapists have learned to utilize that knowledge when working with a client. For example when asking a client what she would like to do differently the therapist looks, or motions in the direction of the future. To motion in the opposite direction tends to be confusing to the client's thought processes.

Why do eye-movements follow such a well-defined pattern? NLP doesn't attempt to provide us with an answer. It seems to be instinctive. Something like eating grass.

Why do dogs eat grass? Why do our eyes move involuntarily in directions directed by our thought processes?

Some things about dogs and human beings are destined to remain in the realm of mystery.

38

About Looking Quizzical

A couple of months ago we baby-sat a miniature French Poodle. Tasha presented herself as a small package of highly intelligent dog. The manifestation consisted of her head and eye movements. As she listened to our suggestions or commands she tilted her head from side to side and narrowed her eyes as though she was struggling to understand our spoken words. Whether she understood anything we said except her name and standard stuff like, “sit, lie down, come and no,” I don't know but I do know that she managed to appear intellectual and sharp. That, along with a sweetness of personality, made us think highly of her. She was an attractive dog.

Last week I attended a 3-hour lecture on Depression and Anxiety. One of the speakers made already-known information interesting by the use of a lot of metaphor, the other one presented facts in a boring way.

I made use of Tasha's signals. As I half-listened to the uninteresting one, the other half of me was experimenting with head movements.

Two or three times in the 45-minute lecture I managed to look quizzical, turning my head on a tilt from side to side and squinting my eyes a bit.

Then as I watched the speaker I began to notice that he was speaking directly to me, as though I were the only member of his audience. And that knowledge brought with it a new interest on my part in what he was saying.

So, Tasha helped two of us. She helped me in an interesting experiment that led me away from being bored to being absorbed in what was going on. And she enabled the speaker to gain a new confidence in the belief that what he was saying was interesting to at least one of his hearers.

39

About Reconciliation

Sometimes I am mean to my dogs. I never strike them but I yell at them to "Get Down!" or "Be Quiet!" and sometimes I bring them up short with a quick jerk on their choke-collar. It is almost always in a situation where I feel that time is of the essence or it's a matter of life or death.

My dogs don't hold this against me. They don't forgive and forget—I think they remember a bit of what they have learned from the action. They do not exercise compassionate understanding for me as I do for them, i.e., understanding what fears motivate abrupt behavior and feeling compassion for the perpetrator. Nietzsche said something about compassionate understanding when he spoke of dealing with the "how" if we know the "why." My dogs don't think in terms of "whys."

But they don't hold it against me. A moment or two goes by and we are reconciled. That is, our friendship is restored, we are in harmony.

I think the essence of reconciliation is the acceptance of things as they are. Dogs are noted for their acceptance of abuse ranging from benign neglect to outright cruelty. In the face of a large spectrum of abuse they remain faithful to the master, and even show gladness with a wag of the tail when they see him coming home. Human beings are not dogs and I do not recommend that people passively submit to abuse. But we can learn something from our canine friends about acceptance of facts as they are.

For several years I studied the Japanese Language. In the preface to my first primer Dr. Nakanuma wrote these words:

> Many students of Japanese Language, particularly American students, say the Japanese language is inconsistent. Very well, the Japanese language is inconsistent and my suggestion to those students is, learn to accept facts as they are; for after all, that is the only thing you can do!

On the wall in my office there hung for many years the prayer of Alcoholics Anonymous:

God, Grant me the serenity to accept the
things I cannot change,
The courage to change the things I can
And the wisdom to know the difference!

The key to reconciliation is the wisdom to know and the serenity to accept what I cannot change. And that is what my dogs do with my behavior. They don't demand that I change it. They accept it.

That's what my dogs have taught me. When I see things I do not like in other people, I can assert my desires that they change and while they are changing, or if they do not change, accept them for what they are.

There can be understanding and harmony even in disagreement!

40

About What is Important

Dogs tend to take care of themselves. That is important. When they itch they scratch no matter whose company they are in. When they wish to eat or want to go outside they bark, no matter who is sleeping or talking on the phone or trying to concentrate on something at hand. In times of urgency, such as a flea-bite or a hunger pang or a full bladder they do what comes naturally, they take care of themselves.

I, on the other hand, have tended to forego urgent internal messages: an itchy nose, or a need for relief from a full bladder or from a boring conversation; in favor of being nice in the presence of other people. I recall visiting a friend recently returned from Japan with twenty-two boxes of photographic slides and enduring watching that slow screen for two hours of sheer disinterest rather than bark, signaling that it's time to break up this party and go home. Perhaps I can let my dog teach me something about taking care of myself.

Dogs, also, tend to take care of their masters or of anyone else to whom they feel they owe allegiance. That is why dogs bark at the approach of strangers. The explanation given by most dog trainers is that they are territorial. That may be true and it is also true that they are protective of human beings who are important to them. I think they see each intrusion as a matter of life or death with time being of the essence in fulfilling their safeguarding role.

So, as I can decide to take care of myself, scratching when I itch, barking when I am in need of some kind of change, I can also take care of other people who are dear to me.

Taking care of other people is sometime called co-dependency, the compulsive need to rescue our friends or relatives from what we fear may happen. And co-dependency is frowned upon by psychotherapists.

The key to this dilemma is to understand the difference in compulsive rescuing and deciding to be of help. When time is of utmost importance or a matter of life-or-death presents itself it is okay to do what is necessary to prevent a disaster.

It is up to the person involved in rescuing to decide whether, when, and how, to do it. She/he is the true authority, objective, or subjective. The one to make the decision.

While my dogs do not go through a decision making process about taking care of themselves or of human beings; rather doing it instinctively, I have learned from them about taking care of my own needs.

Pardon me now. I'm signing off because I have an itch!

41

About What's In A Name?

My dogs have names. First they are known as dogs. Walking my dog daily I see many toddlers who can say only a few words but foremost among them is "doggie" which they say with a joyful anticipation of perhaps coming close enough to my dog to reach out to touch her. Say the word "dog" and many people at once conjure up a familiar muzzle and a wagging tale. A smile comes to their lips as they cast their eyes up and away remembering the warmth and happiness that a dog brought into their lives. Other people, who have had a bad experience with animals, may feel a slight shudder but even they may have a stored-away longing to touch the noble animal.

My dogs have given names. Lacey, and Graham and Ginger, etc. It is amazing how quickly they learn to respond to their given name. Sometimes when Graham is not responding to her own name she will respond jealously, when we call Lacey.

They also have been surnamed by my veterinarian with my family name: Lacey Johns, Graham Johns, etc.

And people have names: Homo Sapiens, Mary, Joe, Samantha; Smith, Thatcher, Jones. And if names are important to dogs, they are even more important to boys and girls and men and women. More, probably, than any thing else except my sexual identity, my name is sacred to me. Shakespeare had something to say about it:

Who steals my purse steals trash...
But he that filches from me my good name
Robs me of that which not enriches him,
And makes me poor indeed.
-Othello

Graham had some trouble learning her name. It may be because there were no distinctive consonant sounds in it. Mrs. Woodhouse wrote that dogs like words with T or CH in them: whaT a good dog; siT, feTch. The sounds in the name, Graham, may be elusive to a dog's ears. In fact it was not until we began calling her GraMMy that she responded positively. Or it may be because we were of a mixed mind about what we should call her. Some of the time we called her Sandy and sometimes we called her Berger. We played with her name. I don't think she liked that very much and I'm sure that people don't like it when their name is used in a joking manner.

A good friend of mine was named Hedges Capers. I ran into him one day at the barber shop and joking with the barber I said, "Are you cutting *Capers* or clipping *Hedges?"* The displeasure on my friend's face was definite and immediate. My own name is Harry David and one reason I go by my initials is because I resented the way my brother's friends used to refer to me as *Affidavit*.

What's in a name? It is not surprising that a child named *Martin Luther* King grew up to be a powerful reformer. Or even that a William *Jefferson* Clinton should become President of the United States.

And have you ever heard of a missionary named Gigi?

42

About Running Crooked

Watch from behind as a dog runs along in front of you and you get a distinct impression that the dog is not running in a straight line. There is the slightest hint of a sidewise movement. It is caused by the dog's back feet being placed in their forward movement, one between the front paws and the other to the outside of the front paws. That is necessary to keep the back feet from stepping on the front feet as the dog runs.

Back in the 50s the United States Navy required all recruits to attend a course called, *Character Education.* The first lecture, as printed in. the text, was entitled, "Honesty is the Best Policy." It began with two questions posed to the class: first, "How many of you believe that honesty is the best policy?" and second, "How many of you believe that honesty is ALWAYS the best policy?" the discrepancy in the number of hands that went up in answer to the second question was said to reflect a basic dishonesty in human nature.

Aside from the apparent inconsistency in the idea that if it is a policy, honesty is not actually honesty, there appears to be another flaw in the statement that honesty is always the best policy. Like the dog's running crooked, a bit of dishonesty is sometimes required to keep us from stepping on our own front feet. Most of us use dishonesty at times in order to boost the self-image of a friend or a spouse.

Professional dog trainers stress the importance of generous praise as reinforcement for desired behavior. Sometimes one must look hard to find a positive behavior pattern to praise when training a dog to obey commands. There are times when the dog's positive response is minimal and it is most important at that time to pick up on the slight improvement and praise the dog lavishly. In fact it may be a bit dishonest to stroke the dog for such a minimal change toward what is wanted. This, of course, raises the question of absolute honesty.

Well, what do I say to a friend who asks my opinion about a new hairstyle or a new suit that does not appear to me to flatter the person posing the question? While I may not carry on about the glorious effect of the new style or the new suit on the person's appearance, in order to avoid stepping on my own feet I, at least, offer some kind of mild complement.

In 1965 I bought a new Ford Mustang. After the purchase one of my friends pointed out to me what a mistake it was to buy such an unsafe and uncomfortable car. He was being honest in his opinion and he left me with doubts about what turned out to be a serviceable and trustworthy car. A few days later he turned up with a new Fiat (FIAT was said to be an acronym for "Fix It All the Time"). I asked him if he had already bought it and when he said that he had, I responded, "It is a fine looking car and I think you'll be very satisfied with it." He smiled and went on his way, confident in his good judgment and happy with his choice of automobiles. All because of my slight dishonesty.

It would be slightly dishonest to say that I gained this concept from watching my dogs run. Instead I say that watching them run reminds me of the discomfort of stepping on my own feet, and gives me some comfort when I tell a white lie to a friend in order to keep from stepping on his.

43

About How Do I Get Fired?

Rags, our English Sheep Dog, was a friendly animal who accompanied any member of the family to any room in the house...except...the front-room where we had a new and expensive rug. We taught him early that the carpet was not for him to walk on nor lie on. He could pass through the room staying on the two feet of hardwood flooring that bounded the carpet on all sides.

Rags learned about boxes very early. That is, he knew what his limits were. He could not leave the perimeters of the property. He could not beg while the family was at meals. He could bark once or twice to announce a stranger at the door. And, he could not walk on the front room rug!

That's not so different from you and me. Every life situation constructs a box, the limits of which are fairly distinct. To move outside the box is to invite cultural anathema. The question I ask to establish what the limits are is, "What is absolutely forbidden if I am to remain a welcomed participant in this structured relationship: my family, my job, my church, my school, my country, my neighborhood, my other memberships and relationships?"

For my job the bottom line may be that I get to work on time, dress appropriately, maintain a friendly countenance and accomplish a standard amount of the workload. For my neighborhood the bottom line may be that I mow my yard regularly, keep the house in decent repair and not park any boats or trailers or R.V.s in the driveway. For my church it may be that I will be shunned if I get a divorce, or have an affair, or drink, or smoke or dance or play cards.

One of the most important things I can do in any situation is to figure out how to get fired. What are the limits beyond which I cannot go without getting consequences I don't want? Once I know the limits I can decide whether I want to accept them and remain within the framework in good standing, or step outside the framework and accept the consequences.

When I know the limits it is easier for me to be myself and still stay within the box that is required.

So long as I stay within the limits I can make my own decisions and take charge of my own life. Rags soon established the limits of the front-room rug. When the family was gathered there he would come in carefully staying on the bare floor boundary, get as close to us as he could, then lie down on the hardwood and place the very tip of his nose on the edge of the rug, as though to test the limits rather than violate them.

So, I too, sometimes test the limits, let my hair grow a little long, be five minutes late to work, or wear an earring in my ear or nose. How far can I go without violating the limits?

Of course, I can decide to step outside the limits, if that is required for me to maintain my sense of worth or my health, or to change some ruling of society that I feel is terribly unjust...and take the consequences of my oppositional behavior.

Life is easier when I know the limits: how I get fired. And yet, most of the improvements in societal structures have probably come about because someone decided to move outside the box!

44

About Our Ancestry: Dogs Or Monkeys?

Monkeys, in their several forms: gorillas, chimpanzees, apes, etc., are seldom referred to as man's best friend. They are clever and rather intelligent. They make us laugh sometimes and sometimes, when we hear of them being utilized in medical science experiments, they cause us to cry. They are even domesticated as household pets in homes combining more adventurous and courageous people than I am. They often are frequented by lice and I suppose they should always be housed in pairs so that they can groom each other. Most of us were pleasantly surprised, recently, when a gorilla 'gave up' a child who had fallen into its zoo enclosure, without harming him.

But for the most part. Monkeys are funny!

Dogs are different. From their beginnings they appear to have lived with human families. They are loving and protective. Just today a friend told me of a dog named Fluffy who belonged to his family and became a hero by grabbing a child by the seat of his pants and pulling him out of a swimming pool where he had fallen. Maybe that one gorilla would have done that, too. The truth is we are not surprised by the dog doing it.

For dogs take human life seriously!

So, what is this about man evolving from monkeys? Aside from their physiques being similar to a human being what other similarities do they bring to bear on the question of evolution? Oh, they recognize symbols and pull the correct levers to release food. They have been known to pile boxes one on top of another to elevate them so that they can reach food placed above their heads. What does that have to do with human qualities?

I'm speaking now of those qualities that we perceive as distinctively human: loving, caring, devotion, commitment, sharing, wanting to be with other human beings. Monkeys, no doubt have love for other monkeys, care for their young, may be devoted parents, share food with their offspring. But notice that those qualities appear in almost every animal grouping caring for their own.

Dogs relate those qualities to the people they live with. They form a symbiotic relationship of loving, caring, devotion, commitment, wanting to be with people. They are like human beings in these distinctive human qualities.

Comparing and contrasting dogs and monkeys, I would prefer to have my ancestry rooted in the canine species rather than in the primates. In fact I'll say it: I believe that human beings sprang from dogs!!!

And then I look at the weird behavior of congressmen and other public officials and I doubt that it could be true. Perhaps it was monkeys after all!

45

About Touching Noses

A black cat named *Spooky* lives up the street from me. She is a friendly cat but I had never noticed how friendly until last spring.

On our daily walks as we would approach the home where Spooky hangs out, I would see her sitting under a car in the driveway, watching our advance intensely.

Several months ago while walking with Graham I noticed the cat following us at a distance. So long as we kept moving the cat trailed along, fifty feet or so behind. When we would stop, the cat would also stop and pretend to be interested in something closer to her. As we continued, she too continued, trailing us, maintaining her distance.

A few days later as we drew near Spooky ran out to within a few feet of the sidewalk and stopped, still watching, and now the object of her fixation was Graham. I stopped at the edge of the driveway and Graham, following her strict training, sat quietly at my side.

Spooky approached to within two feet of the dog, then eased forward and touched her nose to Grammy's nose. She then arched her back against my trouser leg and purred. Grammy wagged her tail.

Soon it became a regular pattern. When Spooky sees us coming, she quickly takes her place close to the sidewalk and as we come up even with her, Grammy sits, and the cat comes out and lifts her face to the dog and they touch noses.

Up until that time Grammy had acted aggressively toward all squirrels, rabbits and cats. Having touched noses with Spooky she became friendly in place of hostile as manifested in her sniffing the cat and wagging her tail.

This speaks to me about dealing with my fears, or at least my shyness.

Particularly at parties. In a large gathering of strangers I, as most people, fear being isolated. Along with Eric Berne, I am not sure *What to Do After I Say Hello.* I fantasize myself standing in a corner, a drink in one hand and a plate of hors d'oeuvres in the other, praying that someone will speak to me, or that everyone will ignore me.

Since we met Spooky I have reinforced my assertiveness. Now, I make a special effort to pick out someone (someone who is probably as shy as I) and speak to them about what a nice party it is or how warm, cold or wet it has been today. Thus opening the conversation, it is surprising how frequently it turns into an enjoyable encounter. I have found that I am even beginning to relish some social gatherings.

One other thing. Grammy's nose is almost always cold and a little damp, as a healthy dog's nose is supposed to be. The cat doesn't seem to mind that. But I find that shy people usually do not have cold noses. In fact, they almost always respond to my overtures with warmth and welcome.

Thanks, Spooky, for teaching me that I can also learn from cats!

46

About Heaven

"Isn't there heaven,"
(She was but seven)
"Isn't there" (sobbing), "for dogs?"
she said.

L. I. Guiney

Davy raises the question that bothers many dog lovers. It has something to do with a soul part of beings that is immortal, that continues on after death. It is painful to believe the traditional idea that animals are different: that in matters of immortality, they have no soul; that they live a relatively short time and then, "pouf" it is all over.

Particularly this concerns those who love certain animals: horses, birds, cats and dogs and want them to have, at least, the same advantages of eternal life that they, as human beings, possess.

A guru of Buddhism, after speaking of reincarnation was asked by one of his followers, "Do dogs live again, perhaps as human beings?"

The wise man nodded, "Yes of course." This was followed by another question:

"What about people; do they return as dogs?"

"Only the best of us are allowed to do that!" was the guru's reply.

Only human beings have souls? From whence did such prejudice arise? I suspect that it comes from spatial thinking: that eternal life necessitates a locale, a place that takes up room. If we allow dogs and cats and horses and birds to have souls it must follow that all creatures, large and small, have the same prospect of eternal life as human beings. That would include animals that are not so lovable such as rats and mice and polecats. And insects, fleas and carpenter ants and termites and yes, mosquitoes! Thinking of living on after death in a space that is also frequented by such pests, robs the human being of much of the joy of anticipating eternity!

Suppose heaven is compartmentalized so that spiders are contained in their own locale, skunks in another, no-see-ums behind an impenetrable screen, alligators and crocodiles in a swamp from which they cannot escape and separated from the quiet lakes where immortal humans are allowed to fish for trout (whose souls, of course, are immediately freed to another form of life).

Where in the world (or out of it) could there ever be enough space to contain all of the forms of life that have lived since the beginning of time? You see, thinking spatially, it is impossible. The establishment of such an astronomically large locale would require the entire universe.

When I look into the beautiful, warm, loving eyes of a dog my thoughts go something like this:

"How could there be created such a magnificent being and then have it snuffed out as though it did not matter?" If I have eternal life, so does my dog, all dogs, and all cats, and all horses and birds and insects and spiders and fishes and, for that matter, why limit it to animal life? All flowers and trees and weeds, etc.

Heaven is not a place. It couldn't be big enough to contain all of the life that has ever lived!

Yes, Davy, there is a heaven for dogs! That is, if there is a heaven for you and me.